LOUISA MAY ALCOTT

Other titles in *Historical American Biographies*

Historical American Biographies

LOUISA MAY ALCOTT

Author of *Little Women*

Karen Clemens Warrick

Enslow Publishers, Inc.

40 Industrial Road   PO Box 38
Box 398   Aldershot
Berkeley Heights, NJ 07922 Hants GU12 6BP
USA   UK

http://www.enslow.com

Library of Congress Cataloging-in-Publication Data

Warrick, Karen Clemens.
    Louisa May Alcott: Author of Little Women / Karen Clemens Warrick.
        p. cm. — (Historical American biographies)
    Includes bibliographical references and index.
    Summary: Traces the life of the well-known author of "Little Women",
examining events prior to and following her emergence as a prominent
American writer.
    ISBN 0-7660-1254-9
    1. Alcott, Louisa May, 1832–1888—Juvenile literature. 2. Women
authors, American—19th century—Biography—Juvenile literature.
[1. Alcott, Louisa May, 1832–1888. 2. Authors, American. 3. Women
Biography.] I. Title. II. Series.
PR1018.W37 2000
813'.4—dc21
[B]   99-36476
                                                        CIP

Printed in the United States of America

10 9 8 7 6 5 4 3 2

To Our Readers: We have done our best to make sure all Internet addresses in
this book were active and appropriate when we went to press. However, the
author and the publisher have no control over and assume no liability for the
material available on those Internet sites or on other Web sites they may link to.
Any comments or suggestions can be sent by e-mail to comments@enslow.com or
to the address on the back cover.

Illustration Credits: Enslow Publishers, Inc., pp. 60, 63, 71; Library of
Congress, pp. 13, 14, 89; By permission of the Houghton Library,
Harvard University/59M-314, p. 21; Courtesy Special Collections,
Concord Public Library, p. 30; Photo courtesy of Louisa May Alcott
Memorial Association, pp. 9, 27, 36, 52, 53, 54, 57, 61, 68, 74, 82, 94,
96, 98, 108, 111.

Cover Illustration: Photo courtesy of Louisa May Alcott Memorial
Association (Inset); © Corel Corporation (Background—*Children's
Round* by Hans Thoma).

Pine River Elementary

CONTENTS

Acknowledgments

My thanks to Lynda Pflueger, who encouraged me to write the query letter for a biography of Louisa May Alcott; to the members of my critique groups, who listened and cheered me on; and to my husband, Jim, who had unfailing confidence that I could write this book.

1

MARCHING OFF TO WAR

O n Friday, April 12, 1861, at 4:30 A.M., Confederate troops fired on Fort Sumter in Charleston, South Carolina. The Union soldiers stationed inside fired back. Divided over the issues of slavery and states' rights, the men of the thirty-four United States of America lined up on opposite sides of the battlefield. The Civil War had begun.

Twenty-nine-year-old Louisa May Alcott, longing for action and adventure, wished she could march off to war with the Union regiment from her hometown of Concord, Massachusetts.[1] She was not satisfied doing the usual things women did for the Northern cause—sewing shirts of Union blue and scraping lint from sheets to use as clean pads for dressing wounds.[2]

So, in June 1861, when the call went out for nurses to serve in Union Army hospitals, Louisa May declared her own independence and applied for a position. At that time, nurses were not professionally trained. Women, around thirty years old, with experience tending the sick, were recruited. Nurses had to provide their own aprons and dresses of black, dark brown, or gray. The only uniform was a red rigolette—a knitted or crocheted scarflike head covering. Each nurse was given a bed, meals, and twelve dollars a month.[3]

On December 11, 1862, Louisa May learned she had been accepted for two months of duty in the Union Hotel Hospital. She was to leave the very next day for Washington, D.C.

"I was ready," she wrote in her journal, "and when my commander said 'March'! I marched."[4]

She packed her trunks with her "uniforms," her brass inkstand, a copper kettle, and information copied from *Notes on Nursing*, a book written by Florence Nightingale, a British nurse famous for improving hospital conditions and the way nurses were trained.[5]

That evening, Louisa May boarded a train for Boston with mixed emotions. Although excited by the chance for adventure, she would miss her family: Bronson Alcott, her father; Abba May Alcott, her mother; and May, her youngest sister.[6] Even as an adult, Louisa May had rarely been separated from them.

This photograph of Louisa May Alcott was taken in 1858, three years before the start of the Civil War and Louisa May's service as a nurse.

On the five-hundred-mile journey between home and the hospital, Louisa May traveled by train from Concord to Boston, then to New London, Connecticut. From New London, she sailed to New York, then boarded another train for Washington, D.C. On the afternoon of her second day of travel, Louisa May spotted the unfinished white dome of the Capitol out the train window. She had arrived and had no way of knowing that the next few weeks would change her life—forever.

The Union Hotel Hospital

At the Union Hotel Hospital, Louisa May was assigned an iron bed in a tiny room with two other nurses. The room had a chair, a wardrobe (a cabinet built to hold clothes), and a tin saucepan the nurses used as a mirror. The drafty room was heated by a fireplace too small to hold anything larger than chips of wood.

The next morning, Hannah Ropes, the woman in charge of the hospital, explained the nurses' duties. It was Louisa May's job to change the patients' underclothes at least once a week, empty used bedpans, and bathe the patients.[7]

Louisa May, shy around strange men, was shocked by the task of bathing the soldiers. Then she remembered one of the reasons she had applied to be a nurse—to have new experiences. So she grabbed the brown soap and cautiously approached "the first dirty specimen she saw."[8] The soldier was an Irishman with a fine sense of humor. Encouraged by his jokes, Louisa May "scrubbed away like any tidy parent on a Saturday night."[9]

Louisa May quickly settled into a routine. She got up at 6:00 A.M. and dressed in her uniform. Then she would hurry through her wards, opening windows. The patients complained of the cold, but Louisa May hoped that healthy, fresh air would rid the wards of the foul smells of wounds, washrooms, and cooking.

After a breakfast of fried beef, coarse bread with butter, and weak coffee, Louisa May handed out rations, cut up food for those who needed help, washed faces, dressed wounds, and took orders from doctors. She dusted tables, sewed bandages, and changed bedsheets until all she wished for was fifteen minutes of rest.[10] On her second full day as a nurse, Louisa May learned that a battle was raging at Fredericksburg, Virginia. Soon the casualties would be arriving at the Union Hotel Hospital. At dawn the very next day, she hurried downstairs to a haunting sight: "In they came . . . ragged, gaunt and pale, mud to the knees, with bloody bandages untouched since put on days before."[11]

Louisa May never forgot some of "the boys" from the Battle of Fredericksburg: Robert Bane, a cheerful teenage boy, who had lost an arm but was eager to get an artificial one so he could rejoin the battle; the twelve-year-old drummer boy, Teddy, who cried alone at night for his best friend, Kit, who had died only after making sure Teddy was safe; and the gentle blacksmith, John Suhre, who had a bullet in his left lung that slowly took his life.[12] As Louisa May wrote the letter John dictated to his brother, she knew the brother's answer would be too late.

After a few weeks, Louisa May requested night duty so she could go out each morning and explore the city. She saw the marching infantry, the lines of army wagons, and the men working on the new white dome of the Capitol. Once, she visited the Senate chamber. Too late for the session, Louisa May boldly sat in Senator Charles Sumner's chair.[13] The Massachusetts senator had been one of the first to urge emancipation—freedom for slaves. When she returned to the hospital, Louisa May recorded all she had seen in her journal and in long letters home.

On New Year's Day in 1863, President Abraham Lincoln's Emancipation Proclamation freed the slaves in the Confederate states—at least in theory. Louisa May believed slavery was wrong. Friends warned her to be careful about what she said on the subject, however, because Washington, D.C., was surrounded by slaveholding states that had remained in the Union, and not all its citizens supported emancipation. Louisa May kept her most radical thoughts to herself but was offended by men who "would put two g's into Negro" and by nurses who "were willing to be served by the 'colored' people, but seldom thanked them. . . ."[14]

Once, while Louisa May played with a contraband baby, the child of a runaway slave, the comment of

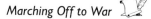

After requesting night duty, Louisa May spent her days exploring Washington, D.C. No doubt she walked up the steps to the Capitol building, where President Abraham Lincoln had been inaugurated on March 4, 1861.

another nurse showed the attitude of many white citizens. The nurse said, "I've been here six months and never so much as touched the little toad with a poker."[15] Even though this nurse most likely supported emancipation, her comparison of the dark-skinned child to a toad indicated that she did not see the baby as a human being. To Louisa May, the color of the child's skin made no difference, and she responded to the nurse's comment by kissing "the toad."[16]

In January, Louisa May recorded in her journal:

I never began a year in a stranger place than this, five hundred miles from home, alone, among strangers, doing painful duties all day long and leading a life of constant excitement in this great house, surrounded by three or four hundred men in all stages of suffering, disease and death. I feel a real pleasure in comforting, tending and cheering these poor souls who seem to love me, to feel my sympathy though unspoken.[17]

Typhoid

During the day, Louisa May continued to explore the city, and then worked through the night in the

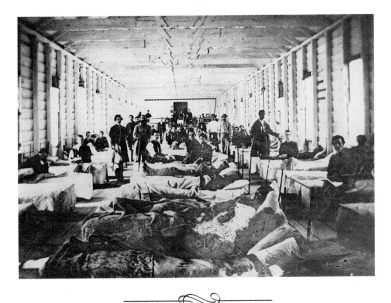

Beds and wounded soldiers lined the hospital ward in Washington, D.C., during the Civil War.

wards. Finally, the bad air, food, and water, with the twelve-hour workdays, took their toll. Louisa May became ill. She even lost the energy to write letters home, but she refused to abandon her duties.[18] She fought dizziness, sharp pains in her side, and fits of coughing until the doctors ordered her to bed.

Louisa May's illness was described as pneumonia or possibly typhoid, an infectious disease spread by eating or drinking unsanitary food or water. She did not improve with medication. In fact, the cure almost proved worse than the disease. The prescribed medication contained mercury, a substance now known to be toxic. Louisa May never completely recovered from the poisonous side effects of the drug.[19] She became delirious and the hospital staff sent for her father, Bronson Alcott. Louisa May was happy to see him but was determined not to go home until she had finished her full term of duty.[20] However, she was too sick to resist.

Mad as a Hatter

Have you ever heard the phrase *mad as a hatter*? Men who made felt hats during the 1800s often used a substance that contained mercury, like the medicine Louisa May was given. Using this toxic substance for years affected the hatters' nervous systems—making them act mad, or crazy. Their speech was muddled. Their muscles twitched and they lurched as they walked.

Bronson nursed his daughter until she could travel. On January 21, 1863, with a basket of medicine, wine, tea, cologne, a blanket, pillow, and the New Testament, the father and daughter began the two-day journey home.

For the next three weeks, Louisa May fought fever and delirium, hovering on the brink of death. After forty days as an army nurse, she had become "a casualty of war."[21]

Hospital Sketches

The letters Louisa May had written home, describing her experiences as an army nurse, were so interesting that Frank Sanborn, a family friend who was editor of the magazine *Boston Commonwealth*, suggested that she turn them into sketches for publication. Louisa May told her story through the eyes of the character Nurse Tribulation Periwinkle.

War Veteran
In September 1863, the Concord troops from the Battle of Gettysburg came home. Louisa May put on one of her hospital dresses, tied her nurse's rigolette over her hair, and joined the cheering crowd that lined Lexington Road. As the troops marched past Louisa May's house, the captain spotted her army-nurse scarf. He commanded his sixty soldiers to halt and come to attention facing Louisa May. The veterans of Gettysburg saluted Louisa May Alcott as one of their own.[22]

Through the Eyes of Nurse Periwinkle

A selection from *Hospital Sketches* showed one soldier's courage and humor. Although the "little Sergeant" had lost a leg and knew his arm had to be amputated, he had this merry moment with Nurse Tribulation Periwinkle:

"*. . . what a scramble there'll be for arms and legs, when we old boys come out of our graves, on the Judgement Day: wonder if we shall get our own again? If we do, my leg will have to tramp from Fredericksburg, my arm from here, I suppose, and meet my body, wherever it may be.*"

The fancy seemed to tickle him mightily, for he laughed blithely, and so did I.[23]

The first of four articles appeared on May 22, 1863. Magazines across the country reprinted the pieces, and Louisa May's mailbox was soon filled with fan letters. Readers were touched by her quiet humor and her simple, eloquent accounts of the men for whom she had cared.

To top off this success, two publishers vied for the right to reprint "Sketches" in book form. After months of illness, Louisa May rejoiced in her first real success as an author. "If there ever was an astonished young woman, it is myself," she wrote, "for things have gone so swimmingly I don't know who I am. A year ago I had no publisher; now . . ."[24]

2

IT'S A GIRL!

It is really not surprising that one of the Alcott children grew up to be a writer. Both parents kept journals and expected their four daughters to do the same. They read constantly and shared stories with their children. What is amazing is that Bronson Alcott and Abigail (Abba) May ever met and married. They came from very different backgrounds with little in common other than the fact that both families valued education.

Amos Bronson Alcott was born on November 29, 1799, in an unpainted farmhouse, patched together from two older buildings. Bronson's mother could barely read or write, but she taught Bronson his letters by drawing them with a stick on the sand-covered floor of the house.

One of Bronson Alcott's first jobs, peddling books door-to-door, led him to his life's work. Often invited to stay in the homes of his wealthy clients, he was permitted to read books in their libraries. As Bronson traveled, he shared all the wonderful thoughts from those books as well as ideas of his own. He soon discovered he had a gift for teaching. By the time he met Abba May, Bronson had developed many of his own ideas about teaching.[1]

Abba May's well-to-do Boston family was one of the earliest to settle in Massachusetts. The youngest of twelve children, she was taught reading, writing, and mathematics by women in a school for young children called a dame school. She also had private lessons in painting, music, and French, and at seventeen, she studied philosophy, arts, and sciences with a female scholar. Abba May met Bronson Alcott when he was invited to her brother Samuel May's home to discuss Alcott's experimental teaching style. Alcott believed children should be taught by exercising their conscience. When children did something wrong, Alcott would ask a series of leading questions to help them think about their actions and feelings. This, he believed, would then help them make a better choice.

Tall and elegant, with chestnut hair and dark eyes, Abba had a character and spirit that charmed those she met. But at twenty-eight, she was considered an old maid, unlikely to marry. Immediately attracted to Bronson Alcott's serene blue eyes and passionate ideas, Abba May recorded in her journal that he was "just the friend I needed."[2] It is likely that getting married was her idea, not his.[3] Bronson, shy and jobless, was torn between his wish to be free to explore his own mind and to have a home and family of his own. But on May 23, 1830, thirty-year-old Bronson Alcott and twenty-nine-year-old Abba May were married.

Germantown, Pennsylvania

In December 1830, Reuben Haines, a wealthy Quaker, read one of Bronson Alcott's essays on teaching and hired him to open a school in Germantown, Pennsylvania. When Anna, Bronson and Abba's first daughter, was born in 1831, the Alcott family was living at Pine Place, a large house surrounded by more than an acre of garden and grounds. It had family quarters and rooms for the school and boarding pupils.

Unfortunately, the family's financial security was short-lived. In October 1832, Haines died, leaving Bronson Alcott without an income. The family had to move to a smaller home. Abba was forced to take in students as boarders. Bronson struggled to keep the school open, but without Haines's support, it soon closed.

On November 29, 1832, during these less fortunate times, Louisa May Alcott was born. As she grew up, Louisa often wished she had been born a boy instead of a girl.[4] However, there was no hint of disappointment in Bronson's letter to Abba's father, Colonel Joseph May: "It is with great pleasure that I announce to you the birth of a second daughter . . . born at half-past 12 this morning . . . on my [33rd] birthday."[5]

For the next year and a half, the family lived together in the Philadelphia area while Bronson struggled to earn a living. Then in April 1834, he decided that he needed to be alone so he could continue his writing. Abba and the girls moved to a boardinghouse in Germantown. Bronson remained in Philadelphia. He made no money while separated from his family, and finally, the Alcotts decided to move back to Boston.

Boston

By this time, Louisa May was an adventurous two-year-old who liked to run away.[6] Later, she related stories from this childhood time in *Poppy's Pranks*—stories

This is most likely a drawing of Louisa May Alcott as a child.

that were not exaggerated. One of the earliest anecdotes happened as the family moved from Philadelphia to Boston by steamboat. The Alcotts had been on board less than an hour when Louisa disappeared. After a long search, she was found in the engine room, having a wonderful time with "plenty of dirt."[7]

Even at this early age, Bronson thought Louisa was a dangerously independent child who had inherited her mother's temper. He suspected eating meat was part of her problem, so he placed his family on a vegetarian diet of plain boiled rice, sugar, and graham meal without butter or molasses.

Such ordinary meals made even apples a treat. To teach the girls the lesson of self-sacrifice, Bronson tempted them with the fruit. He placed an apple on top of a wardrobe, then left. When the girls climbed to go after it, Louisa got there first. But she shared the prize with her sister. Anna felt guilty and confessed to her father, but Louisa grinned and said, "I wanted it."[8]

Bronson did not often spank his children. Instead, he used the withdrawal of his trust and love to discipline his daughters. Anna was sensitive and tried to please her father, but Louisa had a mind of her own.[9]

Love and encouragement accompanied Bronson's strict discipline. Louisa's earliest memories included her father teaching her to trace letters and to copy words. Her first toys were big dictionaries and diaries that she used to build houses and bridges. Her favorite pastimes revolved around books— looking at pictures, pretending to read, and scribbling on blank pages whenever a pen or pencil could be found.[10]

Temple School

Fired up by the new philosophy of transcendentalism, Bronson Alcott opened the Temple School with the help of Elizabeth Peabody, for whom his third daughter, born July 24, 1835, was named. At the school, Bronson tried out his experimental ideas. He used literature to encourage children to think critically. He did not mind if a child politely and logically disagreed with him. His methods for teaching

Transcendentalism

A new philosophical movement called transcendentalism drew Boston intellectuals such as Ralph Waldo Emerson and Bronson Alcott together. Transcendentalists believed in a higher reality—one that rose above, or transcended, what most people were aware of in their daily life. They believed women, no less than men, shaped the world around them through their understanding. The group searched for this reality by investigating how their own minds worked. They studied nature and the great philosophers such as Socrates (c. 470–399 B.C.), whose method of teaching—asking a series of leading questions and nudging students toward the right conclusions—was exactly the approach Bronson had been using.

reading and writing were not commonly used for another hundred years.[11]

Unfortunately, Bronson and Peabody's radical ideas frightened some parents. For example, Bronson was very interested in human birth and encouraged his students to think about it. He then asked each of them to form an opinion on the subject, and in 1836, Bronson published these "sex education" discussions in the first volume of *Conversations with Children on the Gospels* at his own expense and against the advice of Peabody. When prominent newspapers attacked Bronson for heresy, or teaching ideas inconsistent with accepted religious beliefs, parents withdrew many students from the Temple School.

The final act for the school came in June, when Bronson admitted Susan Robinson—an African-American girl. Although slavery had been outlawed in most Northern states and most Boston citizens supported abolition, or freedom for slaves, many did not believe children of different races should attend the same school.[12] Most parents promptly took their children out of the Temple School.

Louisa was an abolitionist like her father, and supported the idea of freedom for slaves from a very early age. Her own experiences, as well as her parents' strong beliefs, influenced her. When four-year-old Louisa fell into Frog Pond in Boston Common, a "Negro" boy pulled her to safety, then disappeared before he could be thanked.[13] Louisa also remembered tugging open the large fireplace oven in their home and finding a runaway slave staring out at her.

Concord

In the spring of 1840, discouraged and in debt, Bronson gave up teaching and moved his family to Concord.[14] With a loan from friend and fellow transcendentalist Ralph Waldo Emerson, the Alcotts rented the Hosmer Cottage for fifty-two dollars a year. Bronson planned to farm the two acres of land surrounding the house.

Louisa remembered her Concord days as the happiest of her life.[15] At the age of seven and a half, she had the run of a many-roomed cottage, the fields, and town. She climbed trees, played hide-and-seek, and performed dangerous feats such as jumping from the barn's highest beam.

The Hosmer barn was a perfect place for plays. Dressed up in Grandfather May's old military uniform or her favorite pair of boots with high soft leather tops that pulled all the way up to her knees, Louisa could play the part of a knight, a pirate, or even a pilgrim when she and Anna dramatized stories.

Louisa and Elizabeth attended school with Emerson's children, and Anna attended a school run by Henry and John Thoreau. Henry David Thoreau, soon to be a well-known writer, used all of Concord to teach the children about nature. Louisa often tagged along on Thoreau's field trips through the woods, swamps, or meadows because Thoreau knew the best places to find animal tracks, arrowheads, huckleberries, and lichen, a crusty fungus that grows on rocks and tree trunks.

During the first Concord summer, Louisa was sent to visit Grandfather May in Boston. When she returned home six weeks later, she found an intruder—a new sister. The baby, born on July 26,

Louisa's First Poem

One cold Concord morning, the Alcott girls found a half-starved bird. Having warmed and fed it, eight-year-old Louisa was inspired to write a poem:

"To The First Robin"

Welcome, welcome, little stranger,
Fear no harm, and fear no danger;
We are glad to see you here
For you sing, "Sweet Spring is near."

Now the white snow melts away;
Now the flowers blossom gay;
Come dear bird and build your nest,
For we love our robin best.[16]

Her mother knew then that Louisa May might have talent and encouraged her to keep writing. Abba's warm encouragement balanced Bronson's reprimands. Poems, impromptu plays with her sisters, and storytelling became outlets for Louisa's independent fantasies.

was named Abba May after her mother. She had golden hair and blue eyes like her father.

Soon after Louisa turned eight, Grandfather May died. Abba, the most needy of his three children, received her mother's silver teapot and a few thousand dollars. But that money was put in trust. Colonel May knew Bronson was not a good provider and hoped to leave his daughter some financial security. He wanted to make sure Bronson did not use Abba's inheritance to pay off the Alcott family debt, later to be known as the "Alcott Sinking Fund."

Abba began to realize that if the family were to survive, she would have to earn money herself. She decided to take in sewing, and she vowed that her daughters would have "trades" and be able to support themselves.[17]

Alcott House

Although his teaching methods were not very widely accepted in New England, Bronson Alcott was greatly admired abroad. A group in

Louisa May's mother, Abba, held the Alcotts together through difficult times, often working to support the family.

England had established a school called Alcott House in his honor. In 1842, Bronson received an invitation to visit the school.

He was delighted and would have set sail immediately—except for the usual problems: no money, family responsibilities, and debts.[18] He asked Emerson for help. Although Emerson had little to spare at the time, he somehow found the money for Bronson's voyage.

Bronson sailed for London on May 8, leaving Abba and the girls alone. Life for the Alcott family was again unsettled, as it often was between Louisa's sixth and tenth birthdays. Louisa matured early and felt protective of her parents, who could not shield their children or themselves from the uncertainties of the world.[19]

3

TRYING TIMES

Abba May Alcott struggled to care for her daughters during Bronson's five-month stay in England. Small sums from Ralph Waldo Emerson and her father's trust helped pay the bills, and friends always brought food and clothing when they came to visit.

In the fall of 1842, Bronson returned from abroad with three new English friends—Charles Lane, Lane's ten-year-old son, William, and Henry Wright. Abba and the girls welcomed everyone, until they learned that these friends had come for more than a visit. They would live with the Alcotts while Bronson and Lane planned a new idealistic

Famous writer and transcendentalist Ralph Waldo Emerson was a friend of the Alcott family. He often gave the Alcotts financial help to get them through difficult times.

community modeled after others located near Concord. Their basic idea was to find more people and create a perfect society. Everyone would live together as one family, the Consociate Family, sharing food, work, and responsibility for the children's education. Bronson and Lane wished to transcend, or rise above, society's problems by creating a community where "honesty, sincerity, and unselfishness and all things of the spirit would rule."[1]

As the men searched for a new "family" home, Abba faced the reality of feeding five children and four adults. A piece of cottage or hearth bread, apples, and potatoes, served on a cloth napkin and washed down with water, was considered a hearty breakfast. When food supplies dwindled, meals were eaten with more and more ritual. For example, everyone would sing a song of praise to God before sipping from the morning's first cup of water.[2]

Excluded from all decision making and forced to follow a strict schedule, Abba found the new plan confining, especially after five months of caring for her girls alone.[3] So she did what she could to make life a bit brighter for the children. On Louisa's tenth birthday, Abba gave her daughter a pencil case to encourage her love of writing. She also invented the Alcott post box. Little notes and packages were deposited in the basket by the door for other family members, then delivered and read after supper.

The Grand Experiment

On June 1, 1843, the Alcotts and Lanes packed up a large wagon and moved fifteen miles westward to a ninety-acre farm at Harvard, Massachusetts. They named their new home Fruitlands. The eleven-member Consociate Family crowded into a dilapidated seven-room house with a kitchen, small dining room, and living room downstairs, and three bedrooms on the second floor for the adults. The children climbed steep, narrow stairs to the attic to sleep. The roof was so low that the girls had to stoop to keep from bumping their heads, but Louisa liked the sound the rain made on the roof.[4]

Shelves were built to hold busts of Plato and Socrates, two famous Greek philosophers, and almost a thousand books that were carted to the farm.[5] Most were about philosophy. Not one book in the collection was about farming, although the Consociate Family planned to grow their own food. Later, one member who stayed for a short time accused the family of preferring literature to agriculture.[6]

Bronson Alcott was a good farmer but was unrealistic at times. For example, he suggested that "The Family" should grow only vegetables that reached toward the heavens, which excluded potatoes, a staple of the family's vegetarian diet.

Strict rules were adopted. Cotton was banned because it was grown in the South using slave labor, wool because it robbed the sheep, and silk because it exploited the worms. All clothing was made out of linen, which was spun from the flax plant. Men wore white trousers and women white skirts. Everyone wore white tunics and canvas shoes.

Extra farmhands could not be hired, and at first, no animals were used to till, or break up, the ground. Later, one family member brought oxen to help with the heavy plowing.

Diet was stricter than before. No meat, milk, or eggs could be eaten. Sugar, tea, coffee, chocolate, and even salt were forbidden. It was an unappetizing diet, and there was never enough food.

Everyone rose at 5:00 A.M. and took what Louisa called "cold baths."[7] These were a primitive kind of shower where water was poured from a pitcher onto the bather. After morning chores, the family gathered for breakfast, often little more than a piece of apple and cup of water. Supper was followed by conversations with the entire family. Bronson or Charles Lane would ask discussion questions such as "What is Man?"[8] Louisa wrote in her diary, "After a long talk we went to bed very tired."[9]

Abba, responsible for all the baking, cooking, sewing, and washing, was soon worn out, even with the children's help. Anna and Louisa learned to fix meals, wash, and iron. Louisa preferred husking corn to ironing and helped all she could.[10] It bothered her to see her mother work so hard. Although only ten years old, Louisa promised herself that she would make her mother's life easier someday.[11]

Life at Fruitlands was an odd mixture of hard work and fun. High-spirited Louisa liked having William Lane for a "brother," someone who would run, climb trees, and play horse with her. And she enjoyed the encouraging notes her mother wrote in her journal.

As the summer began, Anna and Louisa's diary entries made Fruitlands sound like any other family home in the country. But in the fall, things changed. Louisa later destroyed most pages from her Fruitlands journal, but the remaining entries provide clues that all was not well. Louisa recorded that she was happiest when her father and Lane were away preaching.[12] Many entries mentioned quarrels with Anna, fits of bad temper followed by promises to be better. Louisa wrote: "If only I *kept* all [the promises] I make, I should be the best girl in the world. But I don't, and so am very bad."[13] Forty years later, she reread the smudged lines and added: "Poor little sinner! She says the same at fifty."[14]

As Lane and Bronson spent more time away, Abba and the children worked harder. In the fall of 1843, a storm hit when Bronson was not there. Abba and the girls saved the ripe barley by filling laundry baskets and sheets with the cut grain and dragging them to the barn. The barley would be ground into flour and baked in bread to provide food for the winter.

By Louisa's eleventh birthday, only Lane, his son William, Joseph Palmer, and the Alcott family remained at Fruitlands. Lane blamed the troubles on Abba, convinced that she cared more for her own family than for the experiment. He tried to persuade Bronson to leave his family. At first, Louisa did not understand what Lane was suggesting, but she could feel the tension growing and knew her mother was upset. Bronson finally discussed separation with Abba and the girls. Louisa remembered this time in her journal, writing, "Father and Mr. Lane had a talk, and father asked us if we saw any reason for us to separate. Mother wanted to, she is so tired. . . ."[15]

Finally, Abba told Bronson that she and the children were leaving. He could come with them or go his own way—alone or with Lane. Bronson chose to come with them, but the family feared they would lose him anyway. With Fruitlands a failure after only a six-month trial, Bronson went to bed and refused to eat. It was three days before Abba could coax him to drink hot tea and finally to eat. Bronson's hair had turned gray, and he was never quite the same. Abba rented three rooms for fifty cents a week and arranged for the family to move to Still River, Massachusetts, one mile away.

Road Back to Concord

In January 1844, the Alcotts climbed on an ox cart and left Fruitlands. Only thirty-two dollars and the kindness of Still River neighbors kept them from starving that winter. In 1845, Colonel May's estate was finally settled. Abba's inheritance was placed in a trust managed by her brother Samuel May and a cousin, Sam Sewall. Now Abba was guaranteed a small but permanent income. With this money and a bit more added by Emerson, the Alcotts bought a home in Concord less than a mile from Emerson's home along Lexington Road.

On April 1, 1845, the Alcotts moved in. Bronson remodeled the 130-year-old colonial house called Hillside. He added rooms, a porch, and a screened area for the family's cold showers. Abba, finally settled in a home of her own, made money for the "Alcott Sinking Fund" by sewing for neighbors.

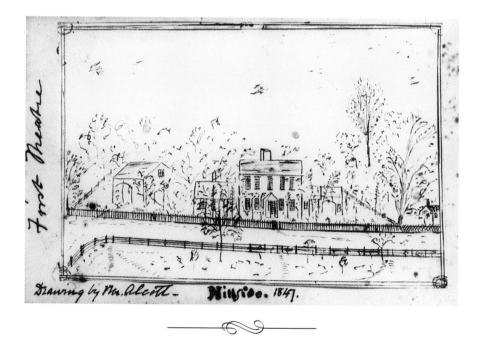

Bronson Alcott drew this sketch of Hillside, where the family moved in 1845.

As Louisa entered her teens that first Hillside autumn, she was growing more like her mother. She had inherited the May temperament and was often feisty and impulsive. Once, she bumped into a chair, and the offending piece of furniture was instantly put on trial, found guilty, and hanged from a window of the house.[16]

Even with their own home, times were hard for the Alcott family. Louisa loved her father, but she realized that he was unable to provide for them. She escaped her troubles by writing in her journal and "Imagination Book," a place for poems and dreams.[17]

The Alcott sisters spent many happy hours at Hillside. It was a grand house for playing "Pilgrim's Progress." With their mother's ragbags on their backs as burdens, they started in the cellar, which was the City of Destruction. They then toiled up the stairs to the top of the house, the Celestial City.

Pilgrim's Progress **by John Bunyan**
This epic story was written while the author was imprisoned for preaching religious ideas that were outlawed by the king of England. One of Bronson Alcott's favorite books, *Pilgrim's Progress* has been widely read since its publication in 1687. Louisa and her sisters had often heard about the journey of the Pilgrim Christian. With a burden on his back, Christian fled his home in the City of Destruction, encountering many trials before finding a safe haven in the Celestial City.

Sometimes the young pilgrims progressed outdoors. Here, they marched up the ridge on the hillside in back of the house and climbed among the trees.

Louisa was the leader in games and adventures. The most popular activities were Louisa's theatricals. She wrote four- and five-act plays that included elaborate sound effects. Louisa and Anna made costumes and scenery and played the main roles. Elizabeth provided musical accompaniment, and both Elizabeth and Abby (young Abba May) played minor roles. All the heroines in Louisa's play were special. They were courageous and attempted brave and dangerous deeds.

A Room of Her Own

At Hillside, Louisa dreamed of a room of her own and shared this wish in a note to her mother, "I have been thinking about my little room, which I suppose I never shall have. I should want to be there all the time, and I should go there and sing and think."[18]

In March 1846, Louisa's dream was answered. Abba fixed up a small room just for Louisa with a desk by the window and a place for her work basket. After she moved into her room, Louisa wrote, "I have made a plan as I am in my teens and no more a child. . . . I have not told anyone about my plan; but I am going to be good."[19] What she meant by "good" was to be more ladylike. Instead of running wildly through the woods, she would sit, sew quietly, and help her mother.

The Hillside days were happy in many respects, but after three years, the Alcott family still had no steady income. Abba began to realize that she would have to be the family breadwinner. In November 1848, just twelve days before Louisa turned sixteen, the Alcotts boarded a train for Boston.

Ralph Waldo Emerson (1803–1882)
Born in Boston, Ralph Waldo Emerson was one of America's most influential thinkers and authors. He followed his family into service as a minister in the Unitarian Church, a Christian denomination, but soon left his post over a dispute. He settled permanently in Concord and lectured in Boston. Emerson's first book, *Nature*, published in 1836, has come to be regarded as his most original and significant work. It explains the basis of his philosophy of transcendentalism.

Emerson encouraged fifteen-year-old Louisa May Alcott to pursue her dream of becoming a writer. He took her work seriously, talked to her about writing, and shared books with her from his own library.

Throughout her life, Louisa acknowledged the influence Emerson had on her life and work. She even had a teenage crush on him. She sat in a cherry tree at night and dreamed about him and secretly left bouquets of wildflowers at his door. Louisa also wrote letters to the forty-three-year-old Emerson, but she never delivered them.

Louisa opened a little school for Emerson's children in the Hillside barn. Ellen Emerson, her favorite pupil, loved fairy tales, and Louisa created a collection of fairy tales just for her.

Louisa did not want to give up walking and running through the beautiful Concord woods or her good friends, the Emersons. She also did not want to give up the room of her own and the quiet she could find there.

But she did have a plan. As one of Louisa May's biographers explained, "The family was not going to be poor forever if she could help it. She put her mind to work."[20]

4

STARTING A CAREER

By 1848, Boston had exploded into a bustling, crowded city, no longer the home Abba remembered from her childhood or even from the Alcotts' Temple School years. The population topped one hundred sixty thousand. Half that number was made up of impoverished immigrants struggling to make a new life.[1]

Abba became one of the first social workers in America, hired by a group of wealthy Boston women to serve as a "missionary to the poor."[2] Pleased with the job, since she was helping the needy while also earning a living, Abba handed out food, clothing, and Bibles. She lectured on cleanliness and thriftiness, took in homeless children, and helped women and men find work. Three evenings a week, with Anna and Louisa's help, Abba taught African-American adults reading and writing.

Life in Boston

The Alcotts moved into a small house on Dedham Street. Their financial situation was actually not very different from that of the families Abba served. Bronson rented rooms at 12 West Street to hold conversations or discussions with others to explore their innermost thoughts.

Abba dealt with family matters. The two youngest girls attended school, while Anna worked as a governess. Louisa May's job was keeping house for the family. It was a monotonous routine, leaving no time for walks or scribbling in her journal. Her view of Boston was through a ground-level window. All she could see was a parade of muddy boots.

When an epidemic of cholera, an often fatal intestinal disease, made it unsafe to stay in the over-crowded area where they lived, Abba's brother, Samuel May, invited the family to spend the summer in his large, comfortable Boston home. With time again to write, Louisa May published a family newspaper, *The Olive Leaf*. Filled with her poems, stories, and articles, the first issue was completed on July 19, 1849.

In the fall, the Alcotts moved back to Dedham Street, and Louisa May helped Anna teach. Work kept her busy. Louisa May had no time alone and she missed it. "I think a little solitude is good for me," she wrote. "In the quiet I see my faults, and try to mend them. . . ."[3]

At seventeen, with her childhood pleasures left behind in Concord, Louisa May stood five feet six inches tall. Her thick, chestnut hair framed a handsome face set with brown eyes. But most of the things that other young women her age enjoyed, Louisa May did without. She did not have pretty new clothes and hats or invitations to parties and picnics. There was not even enough money for the cost of admission to one of the many Boston museums or plays.

Already interested in writing or an acting career, Louisa May used her imagination to escape daily life in the crowded slums of Boston's South End. She wrote plays that the Alcott girls staged and costumed for their own entertainment. Louisa May played the heroes, often juggling five roles while Anna portrayed the leading ladies. They delighted their mother with their quick-change costumes and characters.[4]

As Abba's job became more and more demanding, Louisa May realized that her family was one of many struggling financially. She dreamed of the time when she could provide "a lovely quiet home" for her mother with "no debts to burden her."[5] Finally, Abba could take no more of the long days needed to handle her caseload, as many as two hundred a month. Exhausted, she gave up her job as a social worker.

As their second summer in Boston began, the whole family was exposed to smallpox. The four girls recovered quickly from mild cases, but Abba and Bronson were extremely ill. With no money to pay a doctor or even a nurse, the girls had to care for their parents themselves.

Out to Service

By the time Abba and Bronson recuperated at home, the family fund needed money. Abba opened her own intelligence service, or employment agency. For the next three years, she found jobs for reliable young women as cooks, maids, seamstresses, and dressmakers.

One day, a gentleman from a nearby village came looking for a companion for his ailing sister. He made the position sound delightful. He explained that the companion would be treated as one of the family, required to help only with the lighter housework. The companion would also enjoy the family's books, pictures, and friends. Louisa May thought this job would be more interesting than teaching and would pay better than sewing.[6] She decided to take the position herself. Abba warned her daughter that, although she would be called a companion, she was actually "going out to service" to work for someone else and obey their orders.

Louisa May, sure that the job could be no worse than a harmless adventure, was unpleasantly surprised when the position turned out to be quite different from how it was advertised. She found herself cooking, cleaning, making fires, and running errands. After her morning chores were done, she was invited into the study to listen as her employer read aloud or discussed philosophy. When he began placing notes under her door and reciting poetry as she washed the dishes, Louisa May reminded him that she was there to act as his sister's companion, not his. From that moment on, it was her job to dig paths through the snow, carry water from the well, split kindling, and empty the fireplace ashes. She did everything without complaint until she was ordered to polish the gentleman's muddy shoes. Finally, after seven weeks, Louisa May decided to leave. The sister handed her a small pocketbook, and Louisa May trudged happily toward the station and home, imagining all the things she would buy with her money.[7]

The final act is best described by Louisa May's own words in "How I Went Out to Service:"

> I never shall forget that day. A bleak March afternoon, a sloppy, lonely road, and one hoarse crow stalking about a field, so like Josephus [her employer] that I could not resist throwing a snowball at him. . . . Unable to resist the desire to see what my earnings were, I opened the purse and beheld *four dollars.*
>
> I have had a good many bitter minutes in my life, but one of the bitterest came to me as I stood there in the windy road . . . and looked from my poor chapped, grimy, chill-blained hands to the paltry sum that was considered reward enough for all the hard and humble labor they had done.[8]

When she got home, Louisa May's outraged family returned the four dollars to her employer. Even years later, when Louisa May talked of this experience, the memories would bring tears to her eyes.[9]

During the 1850s, Louisa May explored the few careers possible for women at that time. She tried teaching, but did not enjoy it. She considered acting, an exciting life with immediate rewards, but Abba disapproved. A career on stage was not considered acceptable employment for a refined young woman. So Louisa May sewed to earn money. And while her hands were busy, her mind imagined the wildest and most exciting scenes for stories like "Bandit's Bride," "The Captive of Castile," and "Moorish Maiden's Vow." She also used her work experiences, her family life, and her observations of people and all the things happening in the world

Stick to Your Teaching

Louisa May wrote about her experiences as a servant and her father took the story, "How I Went Out to Service," to James T. Fields, publisher of the highly respected magazine *Atlantic Monthly*. Fields also produced books written by Nathaniel Hawthorne, Ralph Waldo Emerson, Henry David Thoreau, Henry Wadsworth Longfellow, and Horace Mann. After reading her story, Fields kindly but firmly advised Bronson, "Tell Louisa May to stick to her teaching, she can never succeed as a writer!"[10]

This message, she said, made her exclaim to her father, "Tell him I will succeed as a writer, and someday I shall write for the *Atlantic!*"[11]

around her. Louisa May had begun her career as a writer.

Apprentice Writer

Although Fields had done his best to discourage the young author, others provided encouragement. In September 1851, *Peterson's Magazine* published one of Louisa May's poems, "Sunlight," under the name of "Flora Fairfield." Her first story, "The Rival Painters," was published not long after that. Louisa May earned five dollars for it, though she called the story "great rubbish!"[12]

Louisa May realized if she wanted to support herself and her family by writing, she needed to research the publications for which she hoped to write. She studied the stories in the *Saturday Evening Gazette* and other popular periodicals to learn what the editors wanted. On November 11, 1854, her hard work paid off, and Louisa May received an early birthday present. Her story, "The Rival Prima Donnas," was published in the *Gazette* under the pseudonym of Flora Fairfield and earned the author ten dollars.

Encouraged by her first sale, Louisa May kept writing contemporary, passionate thrillers. These stories, published under the alias A. M. Bernard, were often sold to "penny dreadfuls," cheap period- icals filled with gruesome tales of crime and murder.[13] Louisa May liked the easy money these stories earned, but she did not want to admit to

Abolitionists and Slave Catchers

The political atmosphere in Boston and throughout the country was heating up. Louisa May Alcott, an abolitionist from an early age, agreed with those who were disappointed and shocked by the passage of the Fugitive Slave Act of 1850.[14] The new law said that any escaped slaves captured in the North must be returned to their owners. The law was first tested on February 15, 1851. An African-American man named Frederick Jenkins, called Shadrach, who worked in Boston as a waiter, was captured by slave catchers and placed in jail while transportation south was arranged. Before the abolitionists could try legal means to release Shadrach, two huge "Negroes" forced their way into the jail and rescued him.[15] He escaped to Canada on the Underground Railroad, a secret network that helped fugitive slaves reach freedom.

In June, Louisa May watched as another fugitive slave, not as lucky as Shadrach, was paraded along Boston streets before being returned to his owner. Louisa May hoped to see the day "when pistols would be cocked not at the slave but at his owner" and said she would do her part to bring justice.[16]

everyone that she had written such rubbish.[17] As her stories became more popular, editors began to ask for more.

Finally, in December 1854, Louisa May was proud to have work published under her own name. *Flower Fables*, her book of revised fairy tales created for Ellen Emerson, arrived in time to be Abba's

Christmas present. The note the author enclosed read in part: "Into your Christmas stocking I have put my 'first born,' knowing that you will accept it with all its faults (for grandmothers are always kind), and look upon it merely as an earnest [promise] of what I may yet do. . . ."[18]

Louisa May received only thirty-two dollars from the sale of *Flower Fables,* but later noted that she was prouder of that sum than the eight thousand dollars she received thirty-one years later for six months' royalties from all her books published by Roberts Brothers.

In the summer of 1855, the Alcott money had once again run out. The family moved to Walpole, New Hampshire, where one of Abba's cousins offered the family a house rent-free. That summer, Anna and Louisa May organized the Amateur Dramatic Company. Between rehearsals and performances, Louisa May worked on another book, *The Christmas Elves.*

In October, she set out for Boston to sell her book, only to discover it was much too late to publish a book for Christmas. She rented a room for three dollars a week and worked steadily that winter and spring, writing and sewing. Her efforts earned enough to support herself and to send gifts home: a basket of treats and a blanket shawl for her mother, gloves and pretty dress trimmings for Anna and Elizabeth. Her work was beginning to pay off.

5

SAD
GOOD-BYES

In May 1857, with her stories gaining popularity and publishers paying ten dollars for each, Louisa May returned to Walpole for the summer. She was needed to help care for Elizabeth (Betty). The summer before, her younger sister had caught scarlet fever from some children Abba had nursed. Betty had never recovered completely and now weighed only about ninety pounds. Even a visit to the seashore that summer did nothing to improve her health. Fearing their twenty-two-year-old daughter could not survive another cold, snowy New Hampshire winter, the Alcotts decided to move again.

Bronson wanted to move to Concord, where some of his friends had plans for a philosophical college. Betty also wished to live there.[1] With another loan from Emerson, Bronson purchased a farmhouse and apple orchard along Lexington Road for $950. The old house needed remodeling, so the family rented a place in Concord while Bronson fixed up their new home. He enlarged the windows, attached a small farm building on the back, and lowered the floors to make the ceilings higher. He also built bookshelves and niches for the classical busts, reminders of the Temple School days, in the parlor and in his study.

The First Good-bye

That fall and winter, Louisa May devoted much of her time to Betty's care. The doctor encouraged the sisters to continue their homemade theatricals. Betty loved seeing them get ready, and watching the plays lifted her spirits. On her twenty-fifth birthday, Louisa May's journal entry described her feelings, saying, "I lead two lives."[2] She was very happy when involved in the town's social activities or performing plays, then very sad when nursing Betty, watching her die.[3]

When Betty's health seemed to improve, Bronson left on a lecture tour. But her recovery was temporary. By Christmas, she would only allow Louisa May to carry her downstairs and was soon confined to her room. Betty sewed constantly until the last week, when her "needle felt too heavy."[4]

The Alcott sisters enjoyed putting on costumes and taking part in theatrical shows. They sometimes performed in the Concord Dramatic Union, a local entertainment group.

Louisa May wrote that it was "a hard thing to bear, but if she is only to suffer, I pray she may go soon."[5] Bronson was called home in January. There was no more time for amusing plays. Anna took over the household chores while Louisa May and Abba took turns nursing Betty. Betty died on March 14, 1858, at the age of twenty-two and was buried in Sleepy Hollow Cemetery in Concord.

The death of her sister Elizabeth affected Louisa May deeply. She thought of her younger sister as her good shadow, her conscience, and missed her terribly. With a new understanding of sorrow, Louisa May became a different writer—a better writer in her own mind—one who wrote more truly of things she had felt and had known.

Orchard House

Still mourning Betty's death, the Alcotts moved into their new home. Bronson named it Orchard House for the apple trees that stood nearby. Louisa May nicknamed it Apple Slump, in honor of the floors that slanted every which way.

Bronson's study was to the left of the front door. The parlor was on the right. The dining room, used to stage plays, and a kitchen completed the first floor.

Upstairs, Louisa May's room held a walnut bed, a dresser, chairs, and a "half-moon" desk—a hinged board wedged between the two front windows. Bronson built the desk so Louisa May would have a place to write with plenty of light and an inspiring view.

Elizabeth Sewall Alcott, known to the family as Betty, was the sister to whom Louisa May felt the closest. Louisa May was devastated by Betty's death in 1858.

Bronson Alcott built this half-moon writing desk in Louisa May's Orchard House room.

In April, about three weeks after Betty died, Anna announced her engagement to John Pratt, a friend who often took part in Louisa May's amateur productions. The family gave their blessings but asked the young couple to wait awhile. They were not ready to part with another daughter so soon after Betty's death. Louisa May especially mourned the loss of another sister. Although she liked and admired John Pratt, Anna's engagement meant another sad good-bye for her.[6]

In the fall, Bronson and Louisa May left their Concord home. Bronson went west again to lecture, and Louisa May went back to Boston on her "usual hunt for employment, as I am not needed at home and seem to be the only breadwinner just now."[7] Still very upset over Betty's death and Anna's engagement, she was turned away from job after job, and became depressed. Her darkest moment came one evening as she strolled along the bay. Her world seemed to be closing in around her, and Louisa

She Paddled Her Own Canoe
Louisa May herself received a marriage offer about this time. The proposal came from an older man who could provide security for Louisa May and her family. When she asked her mother's advice, Abba wanted to know if Louisa May loved the man. Because the answer was "no," Abba told her daughter not to make such a sacrifice for her family's welfare.[8]

May briefly considered drowning herself.[9] But she was no quitter and her determination was soon rewarded. Louisa May was offered a governess position that paid two hundred fifty dollars a year. Now she knew she could provide art lessons for her younger sister, Abby, clothes for her sisters, and furnishings for Orchard House.

When Louisa May went home for the summer after a successful "third campaign" earning a living in Boston, she decided not to teach anymore.[10] Encouraged by one publisher's praise of her story, "Mark Field's Mistake," and the payment of thirty dollars, she decided to concentrate on writing.

Louisa May had not forgotten that she had promised to write for James T. Fields, the editor who had told her to stick to her teaching. Since Fields was the publisher of *Atlantic Monthly*, she decided to pen a story that fit that prestigious magazine's style. When her story "Love and Self-Love" was praised and accepted by *Atlantic Monthly*, Louisa May was pleased with her accomplishment and the fifty-dollar payment on her twenty-seventh birthday.[11]

Battles Brewing

Rumblings of unrest about slavery continued to stir throughout the nation and even in quiet, little Concord. The Alcotts, schoolteacher Frank Sanborn, and other neighbors formed a society to help fugitive slaves and stop the spread of slavery into the territories. The group invited Captain John Brown, a famous crusader against slavery, to speak at a town hall meeting. His stern manner and enthusiasm excited Louisa May, still a strong supporter of the abolitionist cause.[12]

Sparks continued to fly between the Northern states and the slaveholding Southern states. On Sunday, October 16, 1859, Brown led a small force in an attack on the federal arsenal at Harpers Ferry, Virginia, now in West Virginia. He needed guns and ammunition to lead a full-scale invasion of the South to free the slaves. Instead, Brown was captured and imprisoned. Although Bronson Alcott and Sanborn discussed ways to rescue the abolitionist, Brown was hanged on December 2, 1859.

Louisa May continued to stand firmly against slavery, learning more about the perils faced by fugitives, when John Brown's widow and her daughter later stayed at Orchard House for a month. Louisa

May also heard Harriet Tubman, a former slave and abolitionist leader, describe her many trips leading fugitives out of the South.

A Year of Good Luck

Although almost every day some incident occurred that brought the United States closer to the tragic split between the North and South, 1860 was a time Louisa May called the "Year of Good Luck" for her own family.[13] Anna became Mrs. John Pratt on Bronson and Abba Alcott's thirtieth anniversary. Louisa May, who felt the loss of her older sister deeply, very nearly changed her mind about marriage as she watched Ralph Waldo Emerson kiss the bride.[14]

The author worked throughout August on an adult novel, *Moods*. She had been thinking about the book for a long time and completed a first draft quickly. She also sold another story to

John Brown, the militant abolitionist who was executed for leading a slave rebellion at Harpers Ferry, was considered a martyr by the Alcott family. This portrait of Brown hung in the Alcott home.

In Memorial
Louisa May wrote a poem about John Brown, which was read at Concord's memorial service for him and published the following month in *The Liberator*, a Boston weekly journal dedicated to abolition:

"With a Rose that Bloomed on the Day of John Brown's Martyrdom"

In the long silence of the night,
Nature's benignant power
Woke aspirations for the light
Within the folded flower. . . .

Then blossomed forth a grander flower
In the wilderness of wrong,
Untouched by Slavery's bitter frost,
A soul devout and strong. . . .

No monument of quarried stone,
No eloquence of speech,
Can grave the lessons on the land,
His martyrdom will teach. . . .[15]

Atlantic Monthly. Her reputation was growing. But these successes could not keep up with the family's financial need. At Christmas, there was little money to buy gifts. Instead, the Alcotts exchanged flowers and apples while they discussed the continued violence between slaveholders and those who stood against slavery's spread to the Kansas and Nebraska territories.

In February 1861, Louisa May revised *Moods*, taking time only for a run each evening. Otherwise, she remained at her desk, wrapped in the green and red "glory cloak" with matching silk cap Abba had sewn for her.[16] Her short story sales helped pay the family expenses, but not every manuscript was accepted. When Louisa May submitted a story about a biracial hero in love with a white female abolitionist, *Atlantic Monthly* rejected the piece, fearing that the strong message against slavery would offend too many readers.[17]

This good time for the family also brought Bronson Alcott recognition for his teaching theories. He had served two years as superintendent of schools in Concord and earned a small salary for visiting classrooms, observing teachers, talking with pupils and parents, and writing reports. Louisa May and Anna were in Concord on March 18 for the festival planned

The Kansas-Nebraska Act

The abolitionists had lost another political battle against slavery in 1854 when the Kansas-Nebraska Act passed and opened new lands in the Kansas and Nebraska territories to popular sovereignty, meaning settlers would vote to decide if slavery would be allowed. Abolitionists and Free-Soilers, farmers who did not own slaves or want any slaves in the territory, took up arms against slave owners who tried to settle in the new lands.

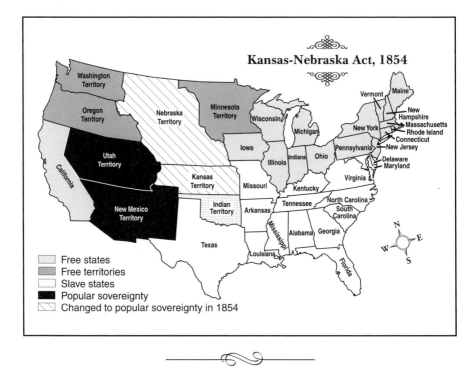

The Kansas-Nebraska Act of 1854, which created the new territories of Kansas and Nebraska and opened them to popular sovereignty in regard to the slavery question, led to violence over the issue of the spread of slavery into the West.

in their father's honor. Louisa May had written a song for the students to sing and as a special surprise, the children presented Bronson with one of his favorite books, *Pilgrim's Progress* by John Bunyan.

Civil War

With Abraham Lincoln's election as the sixteenth president of the United States, the country drew closer to war. In his inaugural address in March 1861, Lincoln tried to preserve peace, but left no

The Alcott family stands outside of Orchard House. It would be the house in which Louisa May wrote many of her most famous works.

Notes and Memoranda 1860
Morning Glories ($)15
A Modern Cinderella ($)75
Debby's Debut ($)50
Monk's Island ($)10[18]
Since Bronson could not support the family and keep them debt-free, Louisa May assumed that responsibility. She carefully recorded her earnings in her journal and applied much of that income to repaying every debt, preserving the family honor.[19]

doubt that he would not tolerate the secession of Southern states to form their own government, which several Southern states had already done. He declared he would use force if necessary to maintain the Union. The Confederate firing on Fort Sumter on April 12, 1861, ended all doubts about what would happen next. Lincoln called for seventy-five thousand volunteers to form the Union Army.

During the next few months, the war went badly for the North. Reports of battles lost and the deaths of so many young men saddened the Alcott family.[20] During this time, one bright bit of news arrived. Anna and John Pratt announced that they were expecting their first child.

Louisa May, stirred by patriotism and her love of adventure, wanted to share personally in the dangers and excitement of the war. She wrote, "I long

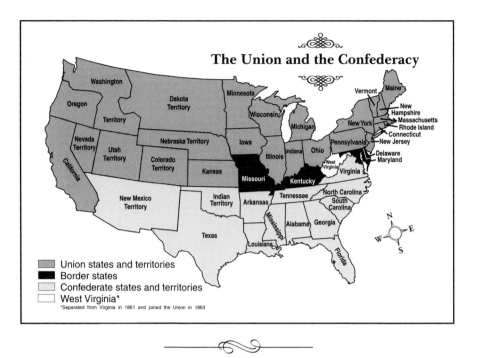

The Union and the Confederacy

Washington
Oregon
Dakota Territory
Minnesota
Vermont
Maine
Territory
Wisconsin
New Hampshire
Michigan
New York
Massachusetts
Rhode Island
Connecticut
Nevada Territory
Nebraska Territory
Iowa
Pennsylvania
New Jersey
Utah Territory
Colorado Territory
Illinois
Indiana
Ohio
Delaware
Maryland
California
Kansas
Missouri
West Virginia
Virginia
New Mexico Territory
Indian Territory
Arkansas
Tennessee
Kentucky
North Carolina
South Carolina
Mississippi
Alabama
Georgia
Texas
Louisiana
Florida

Union states and territories
Border states
Confederate states and territories
West Virginia*
*Separated from Virginia in 1861 and joined the Union in 1863

The Civil War divided the United States in loyalty to the Union and the Confederacy. The Alcotts were strongly supportive of the Union cause.

to be a man; but as I can't fight, I will content myself with working for those who can."[21]

Louisa May spent a year impatiently writing, sewing, and teaching. After seeing a display featuring a six-pound iron slave collar, with three prongs poking out, a rivet in front and a clasp in back, she decided that she no longer could sit quietly at home.[22] It was then that she applied for a position as a Union nurse and was accepted. Suddenly, she realized that she had no idea what the next few weeks would bring and whether she would ever see her family and friends again. She reassured herself that this experience would give her a new focus for all her energies, and she wished to do all she could to support the Union cause.[23] And finally, while she served as an army nurse, only the youngest Alcott, Abby, would be left at home for the family to "feed, warm and worry over."[24]

6

NEW HORIZONS

Louisa May's nursing career ended sooner than planned when Bronson took his daughter home to fight her own battle—against typhoid fever. For three weeks, she drifted in and out of consciousness, tormented by nightmares and memories of wounded soldiers. Her throat was so sore that it was hard to eat and coughing racked her body. Even the comfort of her own bed and her family's tender care could not make Louisa May comfortable.

When the fever broke and she was conscious again, Louisa May learned that her hair, "a yard and a half long," had been cut off, a common treatment at that time for women with high fevers.[1] Doctors believed a fever's heat could actually melt the brain.

Hair was cut short to try to cool the head. Louisa May's legs were also too weak to walk. There would be no more runs through the Concord woods for a while. She had almost died, and in return, she received ten dollars for her service as an army nurse.

During the time spent at the Union Hotel Hospital near Washington, D.C., Louisa May had shared her experiences, and those of the men she cared for, in letters she sent home. When she was strong enough, Frank Sanborn, a family friend and editor of *Boston Commonwealth*, asked her to revise her letters so they could be published.

Since the Alcotts still needed money, Louisa May revised the letters into four articles entitled *Hospital Sketches*. The reaction of readers completely surprised the author.[2] People bought the papers faster than they could be printed, and letters to Louisa May poured into the Concord post office.

It's a Boy

On March 28, 1863, while Louisa May was still recuperating, Bronson came home from Boston with news. Anna's first baby had been born. A boy! Louisa May suggested Amos Minot Bridge Bronson May Sewall Alcott Pratt as a good name for the first boy born into the Alcott family.[3] Instead, Anna and John choose Frederick Alcott Pratt.

With *Hospital Sketches*, Louisa May discovered she had a gift for writing about real life. Although she received only forty dollars for the articles, she said, "They showed me my style. . . ."[4]

Encouraged by the success of *Hospital Sketches*, Louisa May began to revise her adult novel, *Moods*, and planned other stories. She wrote fast and furiously, working so long, without a break, that her hand ached. As she got tired, her handwriting became more and more difficult to read. The author herself sometimes had trouble making out the scribbled words. But Louisa May ignored her pain and fatigue. She had to keep writing. She had to earn money to pay the family's debts.

By the end of 1863, Louisa May Alcott had earned nearly six hundred dollars with her writing and was becoming known as an author. But even her new reputation did not make earning a living easy. The papers and magazines for which she wrote continued to pay the same small fees, and rejected stories with strong antislavery themes.[5] And her best-sellers—blood and thunder stories published under the pen name of A. M. Barnard—Louisa May refused to claim as her own.[6]

In 1863, Louisa May submitted *Moods* to editor James T. Fields at Redpath Publishers. Fields liked the novel but asked that she cut the book in half. Instead, the author submitted *Moods* to another publisher, Ticknor & Fields. It was rejected again. Louisa May then set the manuscript aside until September

1864, when Aaron K. Loring agreed to publish the novel if ten chapters were removed. Louisa May finally agreed to make the necessary cuts and *Moods* was published. At first, the new novel sold well, but when reviewers criticized the work, sales dwindled.

Louisa May spent the first six months of 1865 in Boston. She continued to write, frequently took parts in theatrical performances for charities, and helped her sister Anna when a second son, named John Bridge Pratt, Jr., was born.

Working Holiday

In the summer of 1865, Louisa May was asked to be a companion and nurse to Anna Weld, a sickly young lady, as she traveled in Europe. Louisa May had always wanted to go abroad, and although she was

unsure whether she could fill the duties of a companion, she jumped at the chance.[7] Her family thought it was a wonderful opportunity, but Bronson admitted

Anna Alcott Pratt was Louisa May's oldest sister. Her marriage had been a blow to Louisa May, but Anna continued to be a big part of her sister's life.

The War Ends
Concord went into a week of celebration at the news of Confederate General Robert E. Lee's surrender at Appomattox Court House, Virginia, on April 9, 1865. The Civil War ended shortly afterward, and the Union was brought back together. Only six days later, the celebration ended, and the nation mourned the death of President Abraham Lincoln, who had been assassinated by John Wilkes Booth, an actor sympathetic to the Southern cause.

in his journal that he would miss the income his daughter so generously contributed to the family.[8]

In July, Louisa May, Anna Weld, and Anna's brother George left from Boston. They sailed on the *China*, a ship made of iron instead of wood. People wondered how it could float. Louisa May was slightly seasick most of the way and was glad to step ashore when they docked in Liverpool, England. Louisa May and Anna spent four rainy days in London, then traveled to Dover, England, where they boarded a steamer for Ostende, Belgium. They then traveled to Cologne, Germany, to begin a voyage up the Rhine River.

While floating peacefully along on the river barge, Louisa May took notes about the people, villages, castles, and animals she saw—all to be used later for characters and settings in her stories.

The two travelers from Massachusetts spent most of September in Schwalbach, Germany, while Anna Weld received treatments for her health. Louisa May used this time to walk the paths through the woods and hills, sometimes resting in the shade of the chestnut trees. Near the end of the month, letters arrived from home, letting Louisa May know she was missed.

In October, the travelers moved to a hotel, or pension, in Vevey on the shores of Lake Geneva in the Swiss Alps. One of the other guests at the hotel was a young Pole, Ladislas Wisniewski. Louisa May enjoyed his tales of fighting for Polish liberation before fleeing for his life.[9] His experiences were so much more exciting than Louisa May's daily chores of fetching shawls and pushing her companion about in a wheelchair. Although Laddie, as Louisa May nicknamed her new friend, was twelve or thirteen years younger than she, he was quite likely one of her only romances. Together, they walked in the garden and around Vevey. They sailed the lake, exchanged lessons in English and French, and talked about everything.[10]

After Louisa May celebrated her thirty-third birthday in Vevey, she and Anna Weld moved on to Nice on the southern coast of France, where Anna Weld seemed to rest more and more. The days became monotonous and Louisa May grew restless.[11] After all, she was in Europe, and before she went home, she wanted to see and do as much as

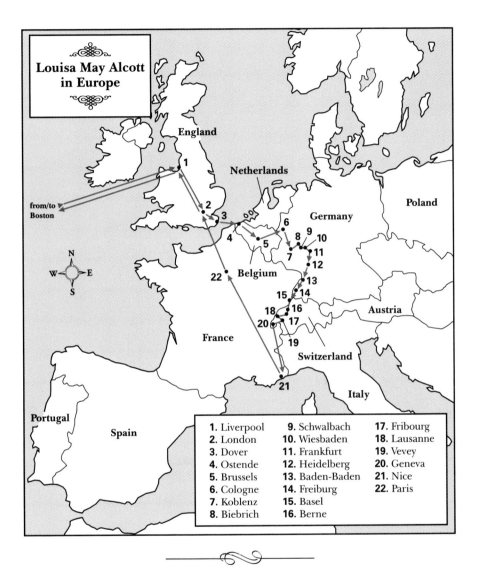

Louisa May Alcott in Europe

England

Netherlands

from/to Boston

Poland

Germany

Belgium

Austria

France

Switzerland

Italy

Portugal

Spain

1. Liverpool
2. London
3. Dover
4. Ostende
5. Brussels
6. Cologne
7. Koblenz
8. Biebrich

9. Schwalbach
10. Wiesbaden
11. Frankfurt
12. Heidelberg
13. Baden-Baden
14. Freiburg
15. Basel
16. Berne

17. Fribourg
18. Lausanne
19. Vevey
20. Geneva
21. Nice
22. Paris

Louisa May visited many places in Europe during her 1865–1866 sightseeing tour.

possible. So, on May 1, 1866, Louisa May left Anna Weld in Nice and traveled alone to Paris. Laddie met her at the train station, and Louisa May spent two weeks seeing the sights with her dear friend.

The final leg of her trip took her back to London. This time she saw the Tower of London, Windsor Castle, and its gardens. She visited the homes of John Milton and Charles Dickens and met with an English publisher about her novel, *Moods*.

Finally, it was time to go home. The voyage took fourteen days and seemed longer, since Louisa May was seasick the whole time. Her brother-in-law, John Pratt, met her in Boston. Bronson waited at the train station. Abba cried when Louisa May arrived at Orchard House. Everyone was glad she was home.[12]

All too quickly Louisa May realized how much she had been missed. While she was gone, the family's debts had grown. Abba had even borrowed money so that Louisa May could spend more time in London.[13] Because the easiest way to replenish the "Alcott Sinking Fund" was to write sensational stories, the notorious A. M. Barnard went back to work.

A Book for Girls?

In September 1867, Louisa May's career took a new direction. She was asked to be the editor of *Merry's Museum*, a popular juvenile magazine. The job, which paid five hundred dollars a year, required Louisa

May's editing skills as well as her contributions of stories, poems, and an advice column. At about this time, Thomas Niles, a partner of Roberts Brothers publishers, asked her to write a girls' book.

Louisa May accepted the job as editor, but it was almost impossible for her to write at home in "Apple Slump." By January 1868, Louisa May moved to Boston and was soon cheerfully writing away in a room of her own.[14]

The task of editing *Merry's Museum* took most of Louisa May's time, and she discovered that she enjoyed writing for young people.[15] For the next couple of months, she concentrated on the magazine job and forgot about Thomas Niles's request for a book for girls.

After two months of satisfying work, Louisa May packed for Concord. Her mother was ill, and Louisa May was needed at home. When Niles again asked her for a girls' book, Bronson urged Louisa May to take his offer seriously. Her father was anxious to please Niles, who had agreed to publish part of Bronson's diaries under the title *Tablets*.[16]

Louisa May was not sure she could write a book for girls, saying, she had "never liked girls or knew many, except my sisters. . . ."[17] But her work on *Merry's Museum* had taught her a lot about writing for children. She knew the writing needed to be simple, that she must never use a long word when a short one would do.[18] So Louisa May sat down at the tiny desk her father had built years ago and began to write her girls' book:

> "Christmas won't be Christmas without any presents," grumbled Jo, lying on the rug.
> "It's dreadful to be poor!" sighed Meg, looking down at her old dress.
> "I don't think it's fair for some girls to have plenty of pretty things, and other girls nothing at all," added little Amy, with an injured sniff.
> "We've got father and mother and each other," said Beth contentedly, from her corner.[19]

After completing twelve chapters, Louisa May sent them to Niles, and although he told her he was disappointed and thought them dull, she worked on and completed twelve more by July. She titled the book *Little Women* and sent it off.

After reading the whole manuscript, Niles was still unimpressed by the story of four ordinary girls growing up during the Civil War. But, because he was a bachelor, he decided to

Abby Alcott drew the cover illustration for the first part of Louisa May's Little Women *in 1868.*

test the story on some young girls.[20] The first to see the book was his niece, Lily Almy. She raced through it and praised it enthusiastically. Niles showed it to a few other girls, and they all loved it. It was different from anything they had read before. *Little Women* was the perfect book for girls.

Niles promptly accepted *Little Women*, making Louisa May an outright offer for the copyright while advising her to keep it for herself. The good advice of this honest publisher was to make Louisa May's fortune.

In September 1868, when Bronson Alcott's *Tablets* came out, Roberts Brothers also released this publicity notice about Louisa May's novel:

> *Little Women*: Meg, Jo, Beth and Amy.
> The Story of Their Lives
> A Girls' Book, by Louisa M. Alcott
> Promised for September 15 at the price of $1.25.[21]

Little Women was actually released on October 1, 1868, in time for Abba's sixty-eighth birthday. The first edition was a cloth-bound book with three illustrations and a cover, all done by May, as Abby, the youngest Alcott daughter, now called herself. It actually sold for $1.50.

Louisa May was pleased with her efforts. "It reads better than I expected," she said. "We really lived most of it, and if it succeeds, that will be the reason of it."[22] But that was not the real secret of her success. Louisa May had learned to write and to write well. All the other stories she had written, all the practice, had prepared her to write her masterpiece.[23]

On October 30, Niles reported that the first edition was sold out. Books were being reprinted and were expected to sell three to four thousand before the new year. *Little Women* was so successful that he wanted a sequel—immediately. By November, Louisa May was back at work, writing a chapter a day, not even taking time to celebrate her own birthday.

From the letters sent to her about the book, Louisa May knew her readers wanted all four sisters to marry. And though the author did not want her representative, Jo, to wed, she finally was forced to create Jo's beau, a German professor. "As if it [marriage] was the only end and aim of a woman's life," Louisa May protested.[24]

Little Women
Louisa May used many of her own experiences in the novel, and readers often confuse what is true with what is made-up. Obviously, Louisa May modeled writer Jo after herself. Amy was an artist like her real sister Abby, or May. All the Alcott girls took part in plays. But Bronson Alcott did not fight in the Civil War, and Laurie was not an American boy. His character was a blend of Louisa May's young Polish friend, Laddie, and Alf Whitman, a Concord friend. Orchard House was the model for the March girls' home. Eventually, the two parts of this popular story were combined into the novel we know today as *Little Women*.

On New Year's Day, 1869, Louisa May sent the final chapters to Roberts Brothers. She hoped it would do as well as the first. The constant work to complete *Little Women, Part Two* had exhausted her, but she was very happy as she rested at Orchard House. The doctor bills from her sister Betty's illness had finally been paid, and with the royalties, or her share of the *Little Women* book sales, Louisa May had paid back every debt the Alcott family owed.[25]

7

FORTUNE AND TOO MUCH FAME

From the moment her book for girls appeared, Louisa May Alcott's life changed. Letters poured in, followed by nearly as many fans seeking autographs or a glimpse of Miss Alcott, author of *Little Women*. Louisa May was too tired to enjoy the novelty of being a celebrity and wrote in her journal, "People begin to come and stare at the Alcotts. Reporters haunt the place to look at the authoress, who dodges into the woods. . . ."[1]

The second part of *Little Women* was as popular as the first, and Niles immediately asked Louisa May for another girls' book. She quickly started *An Old-Fashioned Girl* but had to put the project aside when she became too ill and tired to write. She finally did complete the rest of the story, but it was a struggle: "I wrote with my left hand in a sling, one foot up, head aching, and no voice. Yet as the book is funny, people will say, 'Didn't you enjoy doing it?' . . . I certainly earn my living by the sweat of my brow."[2]

Europe in Style

By 1870, the royalties she earned from *Little Women* had made Louisa May a woman of independent means. About this time, her sister May was invited to go abroad with her friend Alice Bartlett on the condition that Louisa May accompany them. In need of a rest and a change of pace, Louisa May eagerly agreed.[3] It was unusual for three unmarried ladies to travel alone in Europe in those days, but Louisa May had always done pretty much as she pleased, ignoring prim and proper Victorian standards.[4]

On April 1, Louisa May and May Alcott left Concord, dressed in new traveling clothes. Their cowhide boxes were packed with everything they might need on the journey. Anna's husband, John Pratt, escorted them to New York, where they joined Alice Bartlett, and the next day, they "set forth, as young birds will, and left the nest empty for a year."[5]

The voyage was uneventful except for the celebrity treatment the sisters received. Louisa May welcomed a group of little girls who came to her stateroom door. They brought a copy of *An Old-Fashioned Girl* and told her how much they enjoyed it. She received them dressed in her nightgown, too seasick to leave her bed.[6]

They landed in Brest, France, claimed their trunks, and began sightseeing. Artist May exclaimed over the gables, the turrets with storks on them, the fountains, and the ancient churches. As she sketched, a crowd of little boys stood around her, sometimes criticizing her work.

Louisa May often wrote long letters to her mother, sharing all the wonders she saw—the quaint towns with narrow streets and arched gates, ruined castles, and colorful gardens guarded by windmills. She wished that her nephews could see the children in boat-shaped wooden shoes. The girls dressed in blue cloth caps, aprons, and shawls just like the women, and the boys wore funny hats and sheepskin jackets.

In France, Louisa May met an English doctor who diagnosed the lack of strength in her legs as the side effects of the medication used to treat the typhoid fever that had ended her service as an army nurse. The doctor suggested a remedy he called iodine of potash. Since it was simple and pleasant, Louisa May decided to try it. It provided only temporary relief. Nothing seemed to cure her aches and pains permanently.

Louisa May, May, and Alice Bartlett spent a delightful April in Brittany, France. However, France and Russia were on the brink of war, so they moved on to neutral Switzerland and summered in Geneva. In the fall, it was on to Italy so May could study art. Louisa May painted her own vivid picture with words in a letter home, describing their rooms with "green doors, red carpet, blue walls and yellow bed covers . . . like sleeping in a rainbow."[7] Even when she was tired and ached all over, Louisa May enjoyed all the wonderful sights.

Letters from home were always welcomed by the trio. Louisa May especially enjoyed one from Mr. Niles with an account of her royalties—$6,212. She shared this good news with her family, writing, "a neat little sum for 'the Alcotts,' who can't make money."[8] Letters also arrived, requesting that Louisa May write stories for newspapers and magazines. She turned them all down. She had come to Europe for a rest and vacation. She was not ready to write until her year was up.

Louisa May did begin writing sooner than she had planned. While in Rome, she learned that her brother-in-law, John Pratt, had died two days before her thirty-eighth birthday. Louisa May immediately began *Little Men* so that "John's death may not leave Anna and the dear boys in want."[9] When the manuscript was completed, she sent it to her publisher, then prepared to follow it home. It was decided that May should stay in Rome and continue her studies, but Louisa May was needed in Concord. Bronson and Thomas Niles met her at the wharf with news

Anna's two young sons, Freddy and John Pratt, became very close to their aunt Louisa May. She wrote Little Men *to help the Pratts financially.*

of her new book. *Little Men* was just one day old and had already sold fifty thousand copies.

June 1871 was a happy month. Louisa May felt well for the first time in two years.[10] But by the time May returned in October, Louisa May was ill again and went back to Boston to rest and work. Her own words best describe her suffering, "No sleep without morphine!"[11]

And Time Goes by

For the next six years, Louisa May lived and worked in Boston during the winter, trying to meet publishers' demands for more books. She revised her novel *Success* and renamed it *Work*. She wrote *Eight Cousins*, and its sequel, *Rose in Bloom*. Bronson Alcott continued to tour the West, now with a new trunk, warm flannels, neat shirts, gloves, new suit, overcoat, hat, and all. He loved to tell how he was welcomed as the "father of *Little Women*."[12] Louisa May sent May to Europe in 1873 and again in 1876

Cure for the Vapors

Louisa May's reference to morphine, a drug used as a sedative, might suggest that she was a drug addict, but in the Victorian era many women relieved their tensions and pains with laudanum, a solution of opium, wine, and spices. Louisa May chose to call the medication she used for her pain and sleeplessness by the name that described it most accurately.[13]

to finish her studies. Louisa May's only worry was her mother's failing health, and she spent summers in Concord to be near her.

During the winter of 1877, Louisa May worked on a novel for the famous *No-Name Series* published by Roberts Brothers. The books were all written by well-known authors but published anonymously, allowing readers to guess who had written the story. Louisa May was delighted to be asked and used the more dramatic style she had developed in her very first stories published under the pseudonym A. M. Barnard.[14] She was amused when critics and friends alike were sure she could not be the author of *A Modern Mephistopheles*, because the style was so different from her other work. Abba enjoyed her daughter's well-kept secret, though she did wish Louisa May's name were displayed for all to see.

As Abba's health grew steadily worse, only May's letters cheered the household. That summer while sitting by her mother's bedside, Louisa May wrote *Under the Lilacs*. Abba celebrated her seventy-seventh birthday in October. Soon after, Louisa May closed drafty old Orchard House and moved everyone to a home she purchased for Anna in Concord.

Less than a week after the move, on November 25, 1877, Abba fell quietly asleep in Louisa May's arms and died. May was in London when her mother died, "but it was best not to send for her, and Marmee [Abba] forbade it."[15] Abba May Alcott was buried in Sleepy Hollow, next to Betty.

To Louisa May, her mother would always be Marmee of *Little Women*, but, according to the author, the character in the book "was not half as good."[16] "My duty is done," Louisa May wrote a few days after her mother's death. "And now I shall be glad to follow her."[17]

8

YOURS FOR REFORM AND OTHER GOOD CAUSES

———⌒⌒———

L ouisa May Alcott was born a stubborn child with a mind of her own and matured into an unusual woman for her century. In fact, she would likely have adapted well to more modern times.

In the 1860s, well-bred women did not usually work outside the home. But after her experience as a war nurse, Louisa May declared her own independence from society's rules and pursued a writing career.[1] She always respected the work wives and mothers did at home, but she believed women needed to earn a salary to gain the respect of society and decision-making power within their own families.[2]

She also believed women should have the same educational opportunities as men, should be hired for jobs their education qualified them for, and should receive "the same pay for the same work."[3] In the 1860s, few jobs outside the home were open to women. Writing for children or working for children's magazines as Louisa May did when she became editor of *Merry's Museum* was one way female writers could earn a steady income.

Now that women were making a place for themselves in journalism and literature, Louisa May strongly believed they should use not only their creative talents but their practical ones as well. She wrote that women should

> . . . understand the business details of their craft. The ignorance and helplessness of women writers is amazing and only disastrous experience teaches them what they should have learned before. The brains that can earn money in this way can understand how to take care of it by proper knowledge of contracts, copyrights, and the duties of the publisher and author toward one another.[4]

Good Works

Success did not change Louisa May Alcott. As a child, she had been taught the value of giving to those in need. Although the Alcott family had little to spare, they had always shared what they could. Now that she had gained fortune and fame, Louisa May often set aside her writing to give time, energy, and financial support to worthy causes.

And there were many who needed help. Famines in Ireland and political unrest across Europe sent many refugees to the United States in the 1870s. Many of these immigrants made their way to New York City. Often speaking little or no English, men and women found it difficult to find work. They settled in areas where housing was cheap.[5] These city slums soon became overcrowded, and charity provided by churches and individuals could not meet the needs of all these new Americans.

Louisa May had not forgotten her own mother's work in Boston's slums. On Christmas Day in 1875, while on vacation in New York, she visited needy children at a charity chapel, a hospital, and an "idiot house," a home for the mentally ill.[6] She passed out dolls and candy and recorded the children's delight in her journal: ". . . rows of sticky faces beamed at us . . . and an array of toys wildly waved at us, as if we were angels who had showered goodies."[7]

Louisa May also collected barrels of clothing, food, books, and other essential items for a friend who worked with former slaves who settled in New York City.[8] After living their entire lives in bondage, freedom was a difficult adjustment for many former slaves. They struggled to earn enough money to pay for even their most basic needs.

When in Boston, charity work allowed Louisa May to pursue another favorite pastime. She acted in private theatricals to raise money for good causes. One example was the preservation of the Old South Church, where on the eve of the American Revolution, lanterns were hung in the tower to signal the midnight ride of Paul Revere.[9] When a weeklong fair was held to raise funds to save the historic structure, Louisa May took the stage daily and performed the lead role in her own play, "Mrs. Jarley's Waxworks," an adaptation of Charles Dickens's *The Old Curiosity Shoppe*.

Women's Suffrage

Louisa May had grown up surrounded by those who supported reforms from abolition to temperance,

Advice to a Young Writer

Louisa May was always generous with her time when it came to children. She talked to groups of students about her books and writing whenever she could and encouraged one young man with this letter:

Dear Sir, . . . Each must work in his own way; and the only drill needed is to keep writing and profit by criticism. Mind grammar, spelling, and punctuation, use short words, and express as briefly as you can your meaning. Young people use too many adjectives and try to "write fine." The strongest, simplest words are best. . . .

Read all the best books, and they will improve your style. See and hear good speakers and wise people, and learn of them. Work for twenty years, and then you may some day find that you have a style and place of your own, and command good pay for the same things no one would take when you were unknown.[10]

the belief that alcohol should not be consumed or sold. She was also a firm believer in equality for women and women's suffrage, or the right to vote.[11] She applauded the work of Lucretia Mott, Susan B. Anthony, and Elizabeth Cady Stanton, founders of the National Woman Suffrage Association, as they battled to win the right to vote for women.

Louisa May used her greatest talent to support their cause. She wrote letters, articles, stories, and poems for *Woman's Journal,* the only paper published in Massachusetts that was "devoted to the interests of Woman."[12] Her writings clearly show that she believed women should have the right to vote. However, Louisa May also believed voting was a privilege and that all women needed to work actively to win that right.[13]

She also helped the women's movement in other ways. She supported other female writers, encouraged her publishers to print a book on

Louisa May Alcott admired the work of Susan B. Anthony (standing) and Elizabeth Cady Stanton (seated), who worked to win women's right to vote.

the history of women's suffrage, and contributed financial support. Editor and fellow suffragist Lucy Stone remembered one morning when Louisa May arrived at the office of *Woman's Journal* and handed her a check for one hundred dollars. "I made this before breakfast by my writing," she said, "and I know of no better place to invest it than in this cause."[14]

In October 1875, Louisa May traveled to Syracuse, New York, to attend the Women's Congress, a meeting of those actively working for women's rights. When many of the young participants learned that Louisa May Alcott was in the audience, they petitioned the president to invite Louisa May to sit on the platform. She refused to be placed on display but could not avoid being asked to sign autographs and answer questions. Her young fans' enthusiastic admiration was so spontaneous that Louisa May actually enjoyed the fun of being treated as a celebrity.

Louisa May's most challenging battle for the cause of women's suffrage was fought in her own hometown, where a woman's right to vote was an unpopular issue.[15] In 1879, when the state of Massachusetts passed the "Act to Give Women the Right to Vote for Members of School Committees," Louisa May did her best to encourage every eligible woman in Concord to register. She held several meetings in support of the cause in her own home, even though she did not like public speaking.[16]

Women Get the Vote

As early as 1890, the state of Wyoming, newly admitted to the United States, became the first to give women the right to vote in all elections. Gradually, other states began granting women equal or partial voting rights. But it was not until 1920, when the Nineteenth Amendment to the United States Constitution was ratified, that the battle for women's suffrage was finally won. All women who were American citizens were able to vote in a presidential election for the first time in 1924.

She was disappointed with the response and said as much in one of her letters published in *Woman's Journal*:

> I am ashamed to say that out of a hundred women who pay taxes on property in Concord, only seven have as yet registered. . . . A very poor record for a town which ought to lead if it really possesses all the intelligence claimed for it.[17]

This small defeat did not stop Louisa May. She was the first woman to register to vote in Concord; in March 1880, she was the first woman in Concord to vote for members of the school committee.

Her journal entry was brief: "Town meeting. Twenty women there. And voted first, thanks to father."[18] It was a small victory for women's suffrage, and Louisa May Alcott had led the way.

9

FINAL CHAPTERS

With her mother gone, Anna's boys in their mid-teens, and Bronson Alcott enjoying more success with his own career, Louisa May, at forty-five, should have finally had time to think about her own wishes and desires. But the more she helped others, the more they seemed to depend on her. The successful author spent little of her own income on herself. She invested what she could and seemed happy to be able to gratify the wishes of those she loved.[1]

Louisa May spent several weeks with Anna after Abba's death, and she showed no interest in writing or much of anything else.[2] She had not only lost her mother but her purpose in life. The author's motive for all her hard work had always been to make life comfortable for Abba. Now she was gone, and Louisa May missed her terribly.[3] On top of her grief, Louisa May was not feeling well, suffering from many aches and pains. For once, she rested and let Anna take care of her.

In March 1879, some happy news arrived from England.[4] May and Ernest Nieriker, a Swiss businessman, had been quietly married in London. Louisa May, not well enough for a visit to meet her sister's new husband, sent her best wishes along with a wedding present of one thousand dollars. In her journal she wrote: "How different our lives are just now! I so lonely and sad and sick; she so happy and well and blest. She has always had the cream of things and deserved it. My time is yet to come somewhere else, when I am ready for it. . . ."[5]

It is quite possible that Louisa May envied her sister's marriage and happiness, since it had been the older sister's hard work that had paid for May's art lessons and trips to Europe.[6] May appreciated her older sister's generosity and committed herself to becoming the finest artist possible to show her appreciation. Her work was exhibited in a Paris gallery, and the Alcott artist earned thousands of dollars a year by teaching young students and through the sale of her art.

Later that spring, May and her husband, who were now settled in their new Paris home, invited Louisa May to come for a visit. Louisa May was feeling much stronger and wanted to see May, so she made plans to go in September. Sadly, the trip had to be postponed. Anna broke her leg, and Louisa May had to stay home and look after her.

Once Anna was on her feet again, Louisa May went back to Boston. Her mother had been gone a year, and she was ready to write again. She started two new books but found it impossible to concentrate because so many people wanted her to attend parties and perform for charitable causes. In February 1879, she went home. Now she appreciated the quiet life Concord offered.[7]

That summer, Bronson Alcott's School of Philosophy—a place where philosophers practiced transcendentalism—opened in Concord. "He had *his* dream realized at last," Louisa May wrote in her journal.[8] Classes were first held in the study of Orchard House, with Bronson presiding over thirty students.

Bronson Alcott is seated on the steps of his School of Philosophy, a barn-like building that stood next to Orchard House. It was not until later in his life that he finally achieved his dream of running a school that taught transcendentalist philosophy.

The group held conversations to search for a higher understanding of how their own minds worked to shape the world around them. Later a large, brown building was built on the grounds to handle the growing number of students.

About a year after May's wedding announcement, more happy news arrived from Paris. She and her husband were expecting a child. Louisa May sewed clothes for the baby and regretted that she could not be there to help May.[9]

On November 8, 1879, little Louisa May Nieriker was born. The Alcott family received the news with relief and joy that mother May and the baby were doing well. Two weeks later, the joy turned to concern.[10] May, ill with a high fever, was growing weaker daily.

A month later, Louisa May was called downstairs to see Ralph Waldo Emerson. One glance at his pale, distressed face warned her of why he had come. "I found him looking at May's portrait, pale & tearful with the paper in his hand," Louisa May wrote in her journal. "My child," he said, "I *wish* I could prepare you, but alas, alas!" and he handed her the telegram announcing May's death.[11] Ernest Nieriker had sent his message to Emerson, the Alcotts' oldest friend, asking him to break the news as gently as possible.

A letter followed, telling the sad story. The youngest Alcott sister had passed away peacefully on December 29, 1879. May seemed to know what was coming, so she had left directions, packed

May Alcott Nieriker was Louisa May's youngest sister. Her death after giving birth to her first child in 1879 would cause dramatic changes in Louisa May's life.

up trunks to go to her sisters, added entries to her diary, and made sure everything was in order. Her final request probably came as a surprise to both families. "She wished me her baby . . ." Louisa May wrote. "A very precious legacy!"[12] Louisa May's namesake, Lulu, would travel across the Atlantic Ocean to live with the Alcotts in Concord.

Louisa May and Lulu

Until travel arrangements could be made, Lulu was being cared for by her paternal grandmother in Baden Baden, Germany. Louisa May's health problems prevented her from traveling to Europe herself, so, near the end of August, a trusted friend was sent to bring Lulu back.

While Louisa May waited, she finished writing *Jack and Jill*, then put her writing away. At forty-seven, the "mother-to-be" concentrated on preparations for her baby's arrival. She fixed up one of the rooms as a nursery and decorated it with a little white crib.

When Lulu arrived on September 19, 1880, Louisa May was anxiously waiting on the Boston pier and later recorded in her journal: "At last the captain appeared and in his arms [was] a yellow-haired thing in white with its hat off. . . . [She] looked about with lively blue eyes and babbled prettily."[13]

Louisa May held out her arms to Lulu and called her name. The baby went willingly into her aunt's arms, called her "Marmar," and snuggled close.

The Alcotts enjoyed getting to know the happy baby during the next few months. Louisa May found no time for writing or keeping much of a journal as the family prepared for Lulu's first birthday in November. They watched her take her first steps in December.

Her sister's child soon became the center of Louisa May's life. She planned to care for the baby herself, but Lulu was not easy to handle. In fact, her temperament was much like her aunt's. She was stubborn and often threw tantrums.[14] With her continuing health problems, Louisa May could not handle her lively niece alone.

With Lulu to distract her, Louisa May did not attempt a new children's book, but she did look over her mother's papers, hoping to start Abba's memoirs. Thomas Niles had agreed to publish the book. But Louisa May found the memories too painful, and after reading her mother's journals one more time with her father, she destroyed most of

Louisa May Alcott became a mother to her niece, Louisa May Nieriker, or Lulu, seen here sitting on an early version of the tricycle.

them.[15] Louisa May could not write the memoir herself, and she did not want anyone else to try.

The Alcotts had experienced much sadness in the last two years. On April 27, 1882, the family faced another loss—the death of their dear friend Ralph Waldo Emerson.

In October, Louisa May left Lulu with Bronson and Anna and returned to Boston to begin working on a new children's novel called *Jo's Boys*. But she had barely begun to write when a telegram arrived. Her father had had a stroke, and Louisa May rushed home. Bronson seemed to recognize his second daughter, but being weak and unable to speak, he slept most of the time.

While Louisa May nursed her father, she also spent time sorting through her old letters and rereading her journals. She frequently added notes in the margins, making comments on her childhood entries. She burned many pages she believed "not wise to keep for curious eyes to read and gossip-lovers to print by and by."[16]

By April, Bronson's condition had improved, and although he was never active again, he seemed content. Louisa May felt Anna had enough to handle caring for her father, so she took Lulu back to

Missing Pieces

Because she destroyed letters and even entire parts of her journals, there is some speculation that Louisa May may have enjoyed romantic flings other than the one with Laddie. Evidence shows that she was fun-loving, and people who knew her described her as a wonderful woman with a beautiful personality. She was attractive, had a shapely figure, lovely dark hair, and a charming twinkle in her eye. Although she never put herself out just to please people, she did want to be liked.[17]

We are quite lucky to have as much information as we do today about Louisa May Alcott, recorded by the author's own hand. Always a private person, one of her last wishes was that all her journals and letters be destroyed upon her death. Fortunately, no one carried out that request.

Boston with her. She planned to hire someone to watch her niece while she got back to work on *Jo's Boys*. But when she could not find anyone who could handle the spirited girl, Louisa May set her novel aside, and took care of Lulu herself.

Family Ties

In 1884, Louisa May purchased a home in Louisburg Square, one of the most aristocratic neighborhoods in Boston. She moved Anna and her sons, Bronson, and Lulu into the city. Louisa May had also purchased a cottage at Nonquitt, Massachusetts, so the children could spend the summer at the seashore while she and Anna took turns caring for their father.

With her entire family in the same house and no study to call her own, it was difficult for Louisa May to find a quiet place to write. She also discovered she had much less energy. As she worked on the final chapters of *Jo's Boys*, she could write only for an hour or two each day. It is not surprising that her work progressed very slowly, even with Thomas Niles's encouragement.

Finally, *Jo's Boys* was completed and published in 1886. Louisa May was not sure the book was as good as it should be. She recorded her concerns in the book's preface:

> . . . having been written at long intervals during the past seven years, this story is more faulty than any of its imperfect predecessors; but the desire . . . to please my patient little friends has urged me to let it go without further delay.[18]

After the strain of finishing *Jo's Boys*, Louisa May suffered from exhaustion and had to rest. She consulted several doctors, hoping to find a cure for her ailments. When treatments prescribed by feminist Dr. Rhoda Lawrence seemed to help, Louisa May rented rooms at Denreath Place, a nursing home in Roxbury, Massachusetts, to be closer to the doctor.

That summer when she was feeling stronger, Louisa May worked on plans to adopt Anna's younger son, twenty-one-year-old John Pratt. As her legal heir, he would inherit her copyrights when she died. Louisa May also asked that John legally change his last name to Alcott, possibly to insure that the name would continue for another generation.[19]

By the fall of 1886, Louisa May was in constant pain. She complained of dizziness, rheumatism, an ache in the back of her head, and indigestion. She could speak only in a whisper and could not sleep, so she returned to Roxbury and Dr. Lawrence. While under the doctor's care, Louisa May did manage to write a little every day, completing a collection of stories called *A Garland for Girls*.

Roxbury was not far from her Boston home, so she could visit her father frequently. In March 1888, Louisa May went to see him. As they visited, Louisa May realized that Bronson's health was failing, and she was afraid this might be their last time together. She was so concerned as she left Louisburg Square that she forgot to put on her winter cloak.

Louisa May Nieriker
Lulu, at the age of nine, was left motherless again. Her father, Ernest, came to America to visit his daughter soon after Louisa May's death. In June 1889, Lulu went to live with him in Zurich, Switzerland.[20] She lived to the age of ninety-five. Many of her descendants still reside in Europe.

By the next morning, the rest of the family had another Alcott to worry about. Louisa May was very ill, and the doctor could do nothing for her. She complained of violent headaches. John, her nephew and heir, stayed with her until she lost consciousness. On March 6, 1888, Louisa May Alcott died at the age of fifty-five, probably from intestinal cancer, an aftereffect of mercury poisoning.

She died without knowing that her father had passed away two days earlier. News of Louisa May's death reached friends and family during Bronson Alcott's memorial service.

Louisa May had left instructions for her own funeral. It was to be very simple, attended only by family members and a few friends. Her body was carried to Concord and laid to rest across the foot of her parents' grave in Sleepy Hollow Cemetery.

Louisa May's Legacy

During the early 1800s, books written for children were expected to teach a lesson—and that lesson was to be pointed out and explained thoroughly. Most books were dull and boring.[1] When Louisa May Alcott began writing for children, she rebelled against this preachy style.[2] Instead, she showed her readers what she wanted them to understand through her characters' examples. She allowed readers to discover her message for themselves. Children learned something new about the world they lived in just by reading one of her stories.[3]

With Louisa May Alcott's death, young readers lost a valuable ally—one who never forgot what it was like to be a child. However, the author left her dear friends a lasting legacy in *Little Women* and her many other stories.

Louisa May's stories changed the character of children's literature forever and set a new standard for those writing for young readers. Encouraged by her success, other authors followed her example, including details that described children's dress, food, and games. Authors also made children themselves central characters in their stories.

Thirty years after its publication, *Little Women*, the book Louisa May had begun so reluctantly, was listed in the Roberts Brothers catalog as a "noted American classic."[4] With a skill matched by few

Not to Be Read on Sunday

Because *Little Women* did not preach a strong moral lesson in a very pointed way, not everyone praised the book. In a review of *Little Women, Part One*, *Golden Hours Magazine* stated that the novel was not a religious book, ". . . and should not be read on Sunday."[5] It was noted, however, that the book was "lively, entertaining and **not harmful**."[6]

The public disagreed with the magazine's review and by the time *Part Two* appeared in 1869, *Little Women* was unbelievably successful. But public sentiment did not change the opinion of *Golden Hours* and once again the reviewer warned ". . . it is not a book to read on Sunday."[7]

writers, Louisa May wove real-life Alcott experiences and fictional episodes together, making her story fun and lively. Readers still cry when Beth finds Pip, the canary, dead on his cage floor, and they chuckle when Jo throws open the closet door to welcome Laurie as a member of the Pickwick Club. Readers experience life in the 1800s and grow up with Meg, Jo, Beth, and Amy March.

As one reader observed, "She [Louisa May Alcott] unlatches the door to one house, and . . . all find it is their own house which they enter."[8] In fact, Louisa May's characters seem to walk off the page. It is easy for readers to imagine what the March sister would be like if they were to be lifted out of the book and set down in today's world.

Little Women is more than a simple story describing the March family's life. Against the background of the Civil War years, Louisa May identified causes she believed in. She discussed patriotism and abolition, and through the four sisters' everyday experiences, she showed many of the problems women in her time faced.[9]

Although nearly a century and a half has passed since it was first published, her first book for girls is as popular today as it ever was. On the novel's one-hundredth anniversary, a New York City librarian reported that *Little Women* was still one of the two most circulated titles on the library shelves, the other being *The Diary of Anne Frank*.[10]

Around the World

Little Women is not only popular in the United States. It has been published in many countries around the world, including Argentina, Belgium, Brazil, Czechoslovakia, Denmark, Egypt, England, Finland, France, Germany, Greece, Hungary, Iceland, India, Israel, Italy, Japan, Korea, the Netherlands, Norway, Poland, Portugal, Russia, Spain, Sweden, Taiwan, and Turkey, for Louisa May's foreign friends to enjoy.

A Secret Writing Life

For years, no one knew about the blood and thunder tales the author of *Flower Fables* and *Little Women* had written alone in her Boston room.[11] These stories were published anonymously or under one of Louisa May's pen names in story papers like *Frank Leslie's Illustrated*. Although readers loved the passionate stories, Louisa May did not believe these papers, called "penny dreadfuls," were respectable.[12] She once remarked, "No one takes it [Leslie's newspaper] here [in Concord]."[13] In spite of this, Louisa May did admit that she enjoyed writing sensational tales because of "her passion for [a] wild adventurous life."[14]

Louisa May had disguised her "other" writing career carefully. The fact that Louisa May Alcott, "the children's friend," had also written many adult thrillers was a well-kept secret for almost a century.[15] In the early 1900s, as scholars sorted through Louisa May's journals, letters, and manuscripts, they focused on her writing for children.

Finally, some researchers began to puzzle over the cryptic entries in Louisa May's journals and remarks in her letters that seemed to suggest she had penned many other stories. It was not until 1943, when a letter written to Louisa May by publisher James R. Elliott was discovered, that the author's secret writing life was unmasked.[16] The letter identified Louisa May Alcott as the author of many stories published in *Boston Saturday Evening Gazette* and listed the titles of some of her stories and the pen names she used as a disguise. This discovery finally linked the name Louisa May Alcott with A. M. Barnard, and scholars had a whole new Louisa May to study.

Louisa May Alcott had sometimes been criticized for not having reached her full potential as a writer, because scholars thought she "only" wrote for children. Finally, her immense talent and versatility were recognized. Here was proof that Louisa May could write charming tales for children and pen dark tales peopled with villains, vengeful women, blood, and violence.

When researchers Madeleine B. Stern and Leona Rostenberg began digging through back issues of the now-crumbling weeklies of the 1850s and 1860s,

Today, Orchard House is a museum. Visitors may walk through the parlor where the Alcott sisters performed plays and see Louisa May's desk in the room where she wrote Little Women.

they hoped to find more Louisa May Alcott thrillers. But they were afraid many of her tales were lost forever. Fortunately, their fears were not realized. They soon discovered she had written as many stories for her adult fans as she had for children.

In 1975, the first volume of Louisa May Alcott's blood and thunder stories, *Behind a Mask: Unknown Thrillers of Louisa May Alcott*, was published. Today readers can enjoy several collections of stories whose themes include drug addiction, murder, revenge, and the triumph of women over men.

Many of Louisa May Alcott's stories were carried originally by *Boston Saturday Evening Gazette* between 1854 and 1859. The regularity with which they were published indicates how popular they were. These stories taught Louisa May how to write short, entertaining tales. She experimented with many different writing techniques, skills later used as she wrote novels for children.[17]

Toward the end of her life, Louisa May Alcott talked about writing for *Boston Gazette*, saying,

A dozen [stories] a month were easily turned off [out], and well paid for, especially while a certain editor labored under the delusion that the writer was a man. The moment the truth was known the price was lowered; but the girl had learned the worth of her wares, and would not write for less. . . .[18]

Louisa May Alcott was not only the children's friend, she was a professional author who easily penned stories in many genres from fairy tales to realistic war sketches, from gothic shockers to the children's classic *Little Women*. The portrait of Louisa May Alcott was finally complete. Or was it?

Buried Treasure

Scholars have spent years sifting through the handwritten materials left behind by Louisa May Alcott. Every once in a while they are still rewarded with an unexpected treasure. Researchers Joel Myerson and Daniel Shealy made a very exciting discovery during the summer of 1988 while working on *The Selected Letters of Louisa May Alcott*.

While searching individual entries in the card catalog of the Houghton Library at Harvard University, they found the following card: "Alcott, Louisa May. The Inheritance. A. MS.; Boston, 1849. 166p. Unpublished; her first novel."[19]

They were familiar with abbreviations used to catalog materials. "A. MS.," which stood for "autograph manuscript," told them this was a handwritten manuscript. The two researchers recorded the call number and asked to see this piece of the Alcott collection. As they waited, they tried not to get too excited. Only a few days before, information listed on a catalog card turned out to be an empty ledger with a note saying that Louisa May had destroyed the letters.

This time, Myerson and Shealy were lucky. The library assistant brought them "a red notebook, about the size of a student's journal. The handwriting on the blue pages was unmistakable; it clearly matched the letters written by Louisa during her teenage years."[20]

They carefully opened the cover and discovered a slip of paper inside: "*My first novel written at seventeen—High St. Boston.*" Across the top of the first page was the title *The Inheritance Chap 1.*[21]

Myerson and Shealy had found a treasure—a complete, unpublished novel by Louisa May Alcott, and not just any novel—it was her "first novel."[22] Both men knew "that Alcott herself had once held this very manuscript in her hands."[23]

Neither researcher remembered hearing that Louisa May had written a novel as a teenage girl. The title, *The Inheritance,* was also unfamiliar. "Only excerpts of her journals from this period exist, and unfortunately they leave no clues about *The Inheritance....* Written in Boston when Alcott was only seventeen, the work was important enough to the author

Louisa May Alcott is remembered as one of the most successful children's authors of all time.

that she never destroyed it," the researchers explained. "In fact, at some later point in her life, she pasted into the cover the notice that it was her first novel. . . . What we do know is that the manuscript was passed down to Alcott's heirs."[24]

This manuscript turned up for the first time in the mid-1930s when it was loaned to the Orchard House Museum in Concord. It was sent to the Houghton Library to be catalogued and stored with other Louisa May Alcott papers in 1974.[25]

The Inheritance was finally published in 1997. Now readers can share the excitement of Myerson and Shealy as they opened the cover of Louisa May's first novel:

> In a green park, where troops of bright-deer lay sleeping under drooping trees and a clear lake mirrored in its bosom the flowers that grew upon its edge, there stood Lord Hamilton's stately home, half castle and half mansion.[26]

With the discovery of her first novel, another dimension has been added to our picture of Louisa May—a woman who once wondered if people would someday read about her and care about her struggles. And we do, possibly because Louisa May put so much of herself into everything she wrote. We have come to know and love Louisa May Alcott by the pen that was almost always in her hand.

CHRONOLOGY

1830—Bronson Alcott and Abigail "Abba" May married in Boston on May 23.

1831—Anna Bronson Alcott is born in Philadelphia on March 16.

1832—Louisa May Alcott is born in Germantown, Pennsylvania, on November 29.

1834—The Alcotts move to Boston, Massachusetts, where Bronson Alcott starts the Temple School.

1835—Elizabeth Sewall Alcott is born on June 24.

1840—Abba May Alcott is born in Concord, Massachusetts, on July 26.

1843—The Alcotts move to Fruitlands in Harvard, Massachusetts, on June 1.

1845—The Alcotts move to Hillside, a house in Concord along Lexington Road on April 1.

1846—Louisa May Alcott gets her own room in March.

1848—The Alcotts move to Boston on November 17, where Abba goes to work helping the poor.

1851—First poem "Sunlight," under pen name Flora Fairfield, is published in *Peterson's Magazine* in September.

1852—"The Rival Painters" is published on May 8.

1854—*Flower Fables* is published in December.

1857—The family moves back to Concord in October.

1858—Elizabeth Alcott dies on March 14.

1860—Anna Alcott and John Pratt are married in Orchard House on May 23.

1862—Louisa May becomes a Civil War nurse on December 13.

1863—*Hospital Sketches* is published in August.

1865 —Louisa May tours Europe with Anna Weld.
–1866

1868—*Little Women, Part One* is published and becomes so successful that Louisa May begins work immediately on *Part Two* in November.

1869—*Little Women, Part Two* is published.

1870—*An Old-Fashioned Girl* is published; Louisa May and May leave for Europe in April; Anna's husband, John Pratt, dies on November 27.

1871—Louisa May writes *Little Men* while in Europe; One of the first published copies is handed to her when she arrives at Boston Harbor in June.

1875—*Eight Cousins* is published in September.

1876—*Rose in Bloom* is published in November.

1877—Louisa May's mother, Abba Alcott, dies on November 25.

1878—May Alcott is married in London, England, to Ernest Nieriker; *Under the Lilacs* is published.

1879—May gives birth to Louisa May (Lulu) Nieriker in Paris, France, on November 8; May dies in Paris on December 29.

1880—Lulu comes to live with Louisa May in Boston on September 19; *Jack and Jill* is published.

1882—Ralph Waldo Emerson dies on April 27.

1886—*Jo's Boys* is published in October.

1888—Louisa May's father, Bronson Alcott, dies on March 4; Louisa May Alcott dies on March 6.

CHAPTER NOTES

Chapter 1. Marching Off to War

1. Louisa May Alcott, *Alternative Alcott*, ed. Elaine Showalter (New Brunswick: Rutgers University Press, 1988), p. xviii.

2. Ibid.

3. Norma Johnston, *Louisa May: The World and Works of Louisa May Alcott* (New York: Four Winds Press, 1991), p. 144.

4. Ednah D. Cheney, ed., *Louisa May Alcott, Her Life, Letters and Journals* (New York: Gramercy Books, 1995), p. 97.

5. Johnston, p. 142.

6. Kathleen Burke, *Louisa May Alcott* (New York: Chelsea House Publishers, 1988), p. 13.

7. Madeleine B. Stern, *Louisa May Alcott* (New York: Peter Nevill Limited, 1952), pp. 118–119.

8. Marjorie Worthington, *Miss Alcott of Concord* (New York: Doubleday & Company, Inc., 1958), p. 130.

9. Ibid.

10. Cheney, p. 99.

11. Burke, pp. 17–18.

12. Cheney, p. 99.

13. Sarah Elbert, *A Hunger for Home* (New Brunswick: Rutgers University Press, 1987), p. 126.

14. Ibid.

15. Ibid.

16. Ibid.

17. Cheney, p. 98.

18. Worthington, p. 138.

19. Alcott, pp. xx–xxi.

20. Worthington, p. 138.

21. Johnston, p. 149.

22. Ibid., pp. 154–156.

23. Alcott, pp. 24–25.

24. Burke, pp. 22–23.

Chapter 2. It's a Girl!

1. Marjorie Worthington, *Miss Alcott of Concord* (New York: Doubleday & Company, Inc., 1958), p. 16.

2. Norma Johnston, *Louisa May: The World and Works of Louisa May Alcott* (New York: Four Winds Press, 1991), p. 18.

3. Worthington, p. 16.

4. Ibid., p. 17.

5. Ednah D. Cheney, ed., *Louisa May Alcott, Her Life, Letters and Journals* (New York: Gramercy Books, 1995), p. 3.

6. Aileen Fisher and Olive Rabe, *We Alcotts, the Story of Louisa M. Alcott's Family As Seen Through the Eyes of Marmee, the Mother of Little Women* (New York: Atheneum, 1968), p. 56.

7. Cheney, p. 6.

8. Sarah Elbert, *A Hunger for Home* (New Brunswick: Rutgers University Press, 1987), p. 31.

9. Johnston, p. 35.

10. Cheney, p. 12.

11. Johnston, p. 37.

12. Ibid., p. 48.

13. Madeleine B. Stern, *Louisa May Alcott* (New York: Peter Nevill Limited, 1952), p. 10.

14. Worthington, p. 18.

15. Cheney, p. 15.

16. Fisher and Rabe, p. 95.

17. Johnston, p. 52.

18. Worthington, p. 19.

19. Elbert, p. 46.

Chapter 3. Trying Times

1. Cornelia Meigs, *Invincible Louisa* (Boston: Little, Brown and Company, 1968), p. 31.

2. Norma Johnston, *Louisa May: The World and Works of Louisa May Alcott* (New York: Four Winds Press, 1991), pp. 64–65.

3. Martha Saxton, *Louisa May Alcott, a Modern Biography* (New York: Noonday Press, 1995), p. 136.

4. Gloria T. Delamar, *Louisa May Alcott and "Little Women"* (Jefferson: McFarland & Company, Inc., 1990), p. 18.

5. Ibid., pp. 20–21.

6. Saxton, p. 142.

7. Johnston, p. 64.

8. Delamar, p. 20.

9. Ibid.

10. Madeleine B. Stern, *Louisa May Alcott* (New York: Peter Nevill Limited, 1952), p. 37.

11. Delamar, p. 16.

12. Sarah Elbert, *A Hunger for Home* (New Brunswick: Rutgers University Press, 1987), p. 57.

13. Joel Myerson and Daniel Shealy, eds., *The Journals of Louisa May Alcott*, ed. Madeleine B. Stern (Athens: University of Georgia Press, 1997), p. 45.

14. Ibid.

15. Delamar, p. 22.

16. Ibid., p. 25.

17. Ibid., p. 26.

18. Ednah D. Cheney, ed., *Louisa May Alcott, Her Life, Letters and Journals* (New York: Gramercy Books, 1995), p. 28.

19. Saxton, p. 165.

20. Delamar, p. 30.

Chapter 4. Starting a Career

1. Sarah Elbert, *A Hunger for Home* (New Brunswick: Rutgers University Press, 1987), p. 81.

2. Ibid., p. 80.

3. Martha Saxton, *Louisa May Alcott, a Modern Biography* (New York: Noonday Press, 1995), p. 179.

4. Madeleine B. Stern, *Louisa May Alcott* (New York: Peter Nevill Limited, 1952), p. 62.

5. Elbert, p. 89.

6. Stern, p. 64.

7. Ibid., p. 66.

8. Louisa May Alcott, *Alternative Alcott*, ed. Elaine Showalter (New Brunswick: Rutgers University Press, 1988), pp. 362–363.

9. Maria S. Porter, "Recollections of Louisa May Alcott," *The New England Magazine*, vol. VI, no. 1, March 1892, p. 9.

10. Ibid., p. 5.

11. Ibid.

12. Ednah D. Cheney, ed., *Louisa May Alcott, Her Life, Letters and Journals* (New York: Gramercy Books, 1995), p. 44.

13. Louisa May Alcott, *The Inheritance* (New York: Dutton, 1997), p. 185.

14. Saxton, p. 190.

15. Ibid., p. 191.

16. Stern, p. 71.

17. Louisa May Alcott, *The Lost Stories of Louisa May Alcott,* eds. Madeleine B. Stern and Daniel Shealy (New York: Carol Publishing Group, 1993), p. xi.

18. Joel Myerson and Daniel Shealy, eds., *The Selected Letters of Louisa May Alcott,* ed. Madeleine B. Stern (Athens: University of Georgia Press, 1995), p. 11.

Chapter 5. Sad Good-byes

1. Martha Saxton, *Louisa May Alcott, a Modern Biography* (New York: Noonday Press, 1995), p. 213.

2. Joel Myerson and Daniel Shealy, eds., *The Journals of Louisa May Alcott,* ed. Madeleine B. Stern (Athens: University of Georgia Press, 1997), p. 86.

3. Ibid.

4. Joel Myerson and Daniel Shealy, eds., *The Selected Letters of Louisa May Alcott,* ed. Madeleine B. Stern (Athens: University of Georgia Press, 1995), p. 32.

5. Sarah Elbert, *A Hunger for Home* (New Brunswick: Rutgers University Press, 1987), p. 96.

6. Saxton, p. 219.

7. William Anderson, *The World of Louisa May Alcott* (New York: HarperCollins Publishers, Inc., 1992), p. 52.

8. Marjorie Worthington, *Miss Alcott of Concord* (New York: Doubleday & Company, Inc., 1958), p. 96.

9. Ednah D. Cheney, ed., *Louisa May Alcott, Her Life, Letters and Journals* (New York: Gramercy Books, 1995), p. 68.

10. Worthington, p. 102.

11. Saxton, p. 232.

12. Ibid., p. 230.

13. Cheney, p. 77.

14. Myerson and Shealy, *The Journals of Louisa May Alcott,* p. 53.

15. Saxton, p. 232.

16. Elbert, p. 100.

17. Ibid., p. 121.

18. Myerson and Shealy, *The Journals of Louisa May Alcott,* p. 101.

19. Worthington, p. 100.

20. Ibid., p. 123.

21. Ibid., p. 117.

22. Saxton, p. 249.

23. Elbert, p. 123.

24. Ibid., p. 124.

Chapter 6. New Horizons

1. Marjorie Worthington, *Miss Alcott of Concord* (New York: Doubleday & Company, Inc., 1958), pp. 140–141.
2. Madeleine B. Stern, *Louisa May Alcott* (New York: Peter Nevill Limited, 1952), p. 143.
3. Ibid., p. 132.
4. Gloria T. Delamar, *Louisa May Alcott and "Little Women"* (Jefferson: McFarland & Company, Inc., 1990), p. 70.
5. Ednah D. Cheney, ed., *Louisa May Alcott, Her Life, Letters and Journals* (New York: Gramercy Books, 1995), p. 109.
6. Worthington, p. 148.
7. Ibid., p. 159.
8. Sarah Elbert, *A Hunger for Home* (New Brunswick: Rutgers University Press, 1987), p. 139.
9. Stern, p. 154.
10. Joel Myerson and Daniel Shealy, eds., *The Journals of Louisa May Alcott*, ed. Madeleine B. Stern (Athens: The University of Georgia Press, 1997), p. 145.
11. Ibid., 150.
12. Cheney, p. 129.
13. Stern, p. 167.
14. Cheney, p. 135.
15. Delamar, p. 82.
16. Elbert, p. 142.
17. Worthington, p. 191.
18. Stern, p. 174.
19. Louisa May Alcott, *Little Women* (New York: Grosset & Dunlap, Publishers, 1947), p. 3.
20. Stern, p. 180.
21. Ibid., p. 181.
22. Cheney, p. 133.
23. Ibid.
24. Worthington, p. 199.
25. Martha Saxton, *Louisa May Alcott, a Modern Biography* (New York, Noonday Press, 1995), p. 300.

Chapter 7. Fortune and Too Much Fame

1. Joel Myerson and Daniel Shealy, eds., *The Journals of Louisa May Alcott*, ed. Madeleine B. Stern (Athens: University of Georgia Press, 1997), p. 171.

2. Ednah D. Cheney, ed., *Louisa May Alcott, Her Life, Letters and Journals* (New York: Gramercy Books, 1995), p. 148.

3. Cornelia Meigs, *Invincible Louisa* (Boston: Little, Brown and Company, 1968), p. 164.

4. Marjorie Worthington, *Miss Alcott of Concord* (New York: Doubleday & Company, Inc., 1958), p. 221.

5. Myerson and Shealy, p. 174.

6. Worthington, p. 212.

7. Meigs, p. 165.

8. Cheney, p. 163.

9. Meigs, p. 166.

10. Worthington, p. 230.

11. Cheney, p. 193.

12. Ibid., p. 195.

13. Worthington, p. 231.

14. Madeleine B. Stern, *Louisa May Alcott* (New York: Peter Nevill Limited, 1952), pp. 264–266.

15. Myerson and Shealy, p. 209.

16. Worthington, p. 266.

17. Ibid., p. 264.

Chapter 8. Yours for Reform and Other Good Causes

1. Sarah Elbert, *A Hunger for Home* (New Brunswick: Rutgers University Press, 1987), p. 140.

2. Ibid., p. 65.

3. Marjorie Worthington, *Miss Alcott of Concord* (New York: Doubleday & Company, Inc., 1958), p. 283.

4. Madeleine B. Stern, *Louisa May Alcott From Blood & Thunder to Hearth & Home* (Boston: Northeastern University Press, 1998), p. 58.

5. Worthington, p. 257.

6. Ibid., p. 255.

7. Ibid.

8. Ibid., p. 250.

9. Cornelia Meigs, *Invincible Louisa* (Boston: Little, Brown and Company, 1968), p. 170.

10. Carol Greene, *Louisa May Alcott: Author, Nurse, Suffragette* (Chicago: Children's Press, 1984), p. 121.

11. Stern, pp. 144–145.

12. Ibid., p. 147.

13. Ibid., p. 148.
14. Ibid., pp. 150–151.
15. Ednah D. Cheney, ed., *Louisa May Alcott, Her Life, Letters and Journals* (New York: Gramercy Books, 1995), p. 200.
16. Ibid.
17. Stern, p. 149.
18. Joel Myerson and Daniel Shealy, eds., *The Journals of Louisa May Alcott*, ed. Madeleine B. Stern (Athens: University of Georgia Press, 1997), p. 225.

Chapter 9. Final Chapters

1. Marjorie Worthington, *Miss Alcott of Concord* (New York: Doubleday & Company, Inc., 1958), p. 313.
2. Ibid., p. 266.
3. Ednah D. Cheney, ed., *Louisa May Alcott, Her Life, Letters and Journals* (New York: Gramercy Books, 1995), p. 218.
4. Cornelia Meigs, *Invincible Louisa* (Boston: Little, Brown and Company, 1968), p. 177.
5. Worthington, pp. 266–267.
6. Ibid.
7. Joel Myerson and Daniel Shealy, eds., *The Journals of Louisa May Alcott*, ed. Madeleine B. Stern (Athens: University of Georgia Press, 1997), p. 213.
8. Ibid., p. 216.
9. Cheney, p. 225.
10. Ibid.
11. Meigs, p. 178.
12. Worthington, p. 280.
13. Ibid., p. 285.
14. Meigs, p. 181.
15. Madeleine B. Stern, *Louisa May Alcott* (New York: Peter Nevill Limited, 1952), p. 273.
16. Worthington, p. 304.
17. Ibid., pp. 256–257.
18. Louisa May Alcott, *Jo's Boys* (Boston: Little, Brown and Company, 1886), preface.
19. Meigs, p. 184.
20. Cheney, p. 225.

Chapter 10. Louisa May's Legacy

1. Cornelia Meigs, "Introduction to Glimpses of Louisa," *The Horn Book Magazine*, vol. 44, October 1968, p. 548.

2. Ibid.

3. Ibid.

4. John Keller, "Little Women, 1868–1968," *The Horn Book Magazine*, vol. 44, October 1968, p. 519.

5. Ibid.

6. Ibid.

7. Ibid.

8. Madeleine B. Stern, *Louisa May Alcott From Blood & Thunder to Hearth & Home* (Boston: Northeastern University Press, 1998), p. 259.

9. Sarah Elbert, *A Hunger for Home* (New Brunswick: Rutgers University Press, 1987), pp. 142–143.

10. Lavinia Russ, "Not to Be Read on Sunday," *The Horn Book Magazine*, vol. 44, October 1968, p. 522.

11. Louisa May Alcott, *The Inheritance* (New York: Dutton, 1997), p. 185.

12. Ibid.

13. Louisa May Alcott, *The Lost Stories of Louisa May Alcott*, eds. Madeleine B. Stern and Daniel Shealy (New York: Carol Publishing Group, 1993), p. xi.

14. Stern, *Louisa May Alcott From Blood & Thunder to Hearth & Home*, p. 73.

15. Gloria T. Delamar, *Louisa May Alcott and "Little Women"* (Jefferson: McFarland & Company, Inc., 1990), p. 232.

16. Stern, *Louisa May Alcott From Blood & Thunder to Hearth & Home*, p. 85.

17. Stern, pp. 51–52.

18. Ibid., p. 58.

19. Alcott, *The Inheritance*, p. 180.

20. Ibid., p. 181.

21. Ibid., p. 179.

22. Ibid.

23. Ibid., p. 181.

24. Ibid., p. 188.

25. Ibid.

26. Ibid., p. 3.

BOOKS BY LOUISA MAY ALCOTT

Hospital Sketches, 1863

Little Women, 1868–1869

An Old-Fashioned Girl, 1870

Little Men, 1871

Eight Cousins, 1875

Rose in Bloom, 1876

Under the Lilacs, 1878

Jack and Jill, 1880

Jo's Boys, 1886

A Garland for Girls, 1887

Behind a Mask: The Unknown Thrillers of Louisa May Alcott, 1975

A Long Fatal Love Chase, 1995

The Inheritance, 1997

GLOSSARY

apprenticeship—The time a beginner spends practicing a skill, craft, or trade with an adult teacher.

cholera—Name given to an infectious, often fatal, intestinal disease. Symptoms can include diarrhea, cramps, vomiting, and dehydration.

dame school—A place where young children were taught reading and writing by women.

Emancipation Proclamation—Declaration given by President Abraham Lincoln on January 1, 1863, freeing all slaves in the Confederate states that were rebelling against the Union.

Free-Soilers—People who opposed the extension of slavery into the territories and the admission of new slave states into the Union.

Fugitive Slave Act—Act of Congress in 1850 that provided for the arrest and return of runaway slaves when owners presented proof of ownership to authorities.

heresy—A belief opposed to the doctrines of a church.

humanities—The branch of learning concerned with literature, history, and philosophy.

Kansas-Nebraska Act—Law passed in 1854 that included a provision that allowed the question of slavery in these two new territories to be decided by the settlers rather than by Congress.

martyrdom—How someone is remembered after suffering and dying for a cause.

Missouri Compromise—Agreement that all land in the Louisiana Purchase north of 36°30' latitude, except for the state of Missouri, was to be free of slavery.

mulatto—Person of mixed white and black descent.

pension—European hotel or boardinghouse.

philosophy—Search for wisdom or knowledge.

ritual—A practice done at regular intervals.

typhoid—A serious disease caused by eating or drinking contaminated food or water. The symptoms include high fever, coughing, and red rashes.

Underground Railroad—A system set up before the Civil War to help fugitive slaves escape to free states in the North and Canada.

FURTHER READING

Books

Freedman, Russell. *Lincoln: A Photobiography*. New York: Clarion Books, 1987.

Kendall, Martha E. *Susan B. Anthony: Voice for Women's Voting Rights*. Springfield, N.J.: Enslow Publishers, Inc., 1997.

MacDonald, Ruth K. *Louisa May Alcott*. Old Tappan, N.J.: MacMillan Library Reference, 1983.

Meigs, Cornelia. *Invincible Louisa: The Story of Louisa May Alcott*. Boston: Little, Brown and Company, 1968.

Murphy, Jim. *The Boy's War*. New York: Clarion Books, 1990.

Myerson, Joel and Daniel Shealy, eds. *The Journals of Louisa May Alcott*. Athens: The University of Georgia Press, 1997.

Stern, Madeleine B., ed. *The Selected Letters of Louisa May Alcott*. Athens: The University of Georgia Press, 1995.

Internet Addresses

AlcottWeb–A Site for Louisa May Alcott. <http://www.alcottweb.com/>.

The Concord, MA, USA Homepage. 1997. <http://www.concordma.com/arts.html>.

Orchard House. 1997. <http://www.louisamayalcott.org>.

INDEX